A Bloomsbury Ingénue

Henry Lamb, *Head of a Girl*, *c*. 1907, charcoal on paper, 22.5 x 24 cm

A
Bloomsbury
Ingénue

THE LIVES
AND
LOVES
OF
EUPHEMIA
LAMB

Andrea Obholzer

UNICORN

My candle burns at both ends;
It will not last the night;
But ah, my foes, and oh, my friends –
It gives a lovely light

Edna St Vincent Millay,
from *A Few Figs from Thistles* (1920)

Contents

Cast of Characters

Euphemia Lamb – artist's model, wife of Henry Lamb. Also known as **Nina Forrest**.

Florinda – fictional character based on Euphemia in Virginia Woolf's *Jacob's Room*

Odile – fictional character based on Euphemia in Henri-Pierre Roché's *Jules et Jim*

Pamela – fictional character based on Euphemia in Franz Hessel's *Romance Parisienne*

Anastasya – fictional character based on Euphemia in Wyndham Lewis's *Tarr*

Lobelia – Augustus John's nickname for Euphemia

Max Beerbohm – artist, writer, friend of Augustus John

Clive Bell – writer, husband of Vanessa Stephen, Bloomsbury member

Aleister Crowley – occultist, writer, mountaineer, lover of Euphemia

Sergei Diaghilev – Russian impresario, friend of Henri-Pierre Roché and Nikolai Semenov

Francis Dodd – artist, mentor of Henry Lamb

Jacob Epstein – American sculptor, friend of Euphemia

Prince George – Russian prince, lover of Euphemia

Duncan Grant – artist, lover of Euphemia, Lytton Strachey and Vanessa Stephen

Rudolph Grossman – German artist, lover of Euphemia

Ned Grove – second husband of Euphemia

Franz Hessel – Austrian writer, lover of Euphemia

Lotte/Lucie – fictional version of Franz Hessel's girlfriend Giselle

James Dickson Innes – artist, lover of Euphemia

Augustus John – artist, friend and lover of Euphemia

Gwen John – painter, sister of Augustus John

Ida John – wife of Augustus John

Viva King – friend of Euphemia

Henry Lamb – artist and first husband of Euphemia

Walter Lamb – brother of Henry Lamb and friend of the Stephen family

Percy Wyndham Lewis – artist, writer, friend and neighbour of Euphemia

Caitlin MacNamara – daughter of Francis MacNamara

Francis MacNamara – lover of Euphemia

Nicolette MacNamara – daughter of Francis MacNamara

Ambrose McEvoy – artist, friend of Euphemia

Dorelia McNeill – mistress of Augustus John and Henry Lamb

Edie McNeill – sister of Dorelia McNeill, lover of Henry Lamb, wife of Francis MacNamara

William Molard – French musician, neighbour of Rudolph Grossman and Paul Gauguin

Ottoline Morrell – socialite, lover of Henry Lamb, Bloomsbury member

Victor Neuburg – poet, acolyte of Aleister Crowley, lover of Euphemia, publisher of Dylan Thomas

Maresco Pearce – artist, lover of Euphemia

The Puritans – wealthy American couple

Henri-Pierre Roché – French writer, lover of Euphemia

Morton Sands – American art collector, friend and benefactor of Euphemia

Thomas Scott-Ellis – Baron de Walden, lover of Euphemia

Nikolai Semenov – Russian ballet director, friend and lover of Euphemia

Gertrude Stein – writer, American art collector, friend of Henri-Pierre Roché

Adrian Stephen – brother of Vanessa and Virginia Stephen, friend of Henry Lamb and Nina Forrest

Thoby Stephen – brother of Vanessa and Virginia Stephen, friend of Henry Lamb and Nina Forrest

Vanessa Stephen – (also known as Vanessa Bell), artist, friend of Henry Lamb and Nina Forrest

Virginia Stephen – (also known as Virginia Woolf), writer, friend of Henry Lamb and Nina Forrest

Lytton Strachey – writer, Bloomsbury member

Edmund Spencer Turton – lover of Euphemia, father of Euphemia's son

Leonard Woolf – publisher, husband of Virginia Stephen, Bloomsbury member

Franz Hessel, photograph of Euphemia reading, Holland, August 1907

Introduction

*She did everything in the world
with her determination and her finesse
and even her beauty.* – Henri-Pierre Roché

EUPHEMIA LIVED AN EXTRAORDINARY LIFE; she was catapulted into bohemian London as a teenager from working class Manchester. She capitalised on her beauty and personality to make her presence known in this avant-garde artistic milieu. Her elopement with Henry Lamb spurred her on to become an artist's model; Euphemia inspired many different artists and those who drew and painted her regularly were able to capture different versions of her. This chameleon-like quality extended into her private life and she was able to have many relationships consecutively and concurrently with artists, writers and other lovers.

Still known as Nina Forrest, Euphemia's arrival in London in 1905 brought her into the orbit of the embryonic Bloomsbury Group, who were fascinated by her and Henry. From them and the regular Friday Club evenings, she learned about art and ideas. She was a regular visitor at 46 Gordon Square and would have been privy to their intellectual talk and gossip. Euphemia was a fabulist; she had a wonderful imagination and could create alternative versions of herself, which she did regularly. Virginia Woolf was both enthralled and appalled by her, and this inherent contradiction that a person could be both one thing and another, a princess and a harlot, found its way into her characterisation of Florinda in her 1922 novel *Jacob's Room*.

In 1907 Euphemia went to Paris, where she became known to some of the esteemed writers and thinkers of the early twentieth century. After Henry Lamb abandoned her, she had a brief fling with Duncan Grant and then formed a threesome with Henri-Pierre Roché and his best friend Franz Hessel, which was immortalised in Roché's novel, *Jules et Jim*.

Henri-Pierre Roché tutored her in French and he recommended novels for her to read, including the Russian classics that were then becoming available in translation. He also emancipated her sexually and accepted her having other lovers. Euphemia was fortunate enough to be at the heart of the demi-monde of both English, French and émigré Russian cultural life during the Belle Epoque. It was Roché who introduced Gertrude Stein to Picasso. Euphemia would have been aware of the French painters who dominated at the turn of the century – Matisse, Cézanne and Gauguin.

Euphemia worked as an artist's model for her husband Henry Lamb, Augustus John and James Dickson Innes. Duncan Grant, Vanessa Bell, Jacob Epstein, Ambrose McEvoy, Charles Winzer, William Orpen, Maresco Pearce, Edna Clarke Hall and Randolph Schwabe all used her as a model. There are over seventy known art works featuring Euphemia Lamb. That we have so many portraits of her by a wide variety of artists enables us to build up a visual picture of Euphemia. Her period in Paris coincided with the explosion of modern art. That she also inspired many writers of the period and made her way into fictional characters enables us to build up a fuller picture of her and her personality and guile.

She became embroiled in a love triangle with the occultist Aleister Crowley and his acolyte Victor Neuburg. She became a café star in Paris and attracted wealthy American and Russian lovers. When her life began to spiral out of control, a friend paid off her debts and she returned to London where she set about making herself a lady. She installed herself as a hostess at the Café Royal and courted rich and powerful men, aristocrats and politicians as well as artists. By the end of her life she lived in the country and had an impressive art collection, and her son went to Eton and Oxford.

The women of Montparnasse 'helped create a new era with no hypocrisy, living an honest, natural and unprejudiced life'.[1]

---

1. Peter Brooker, *Bohemia in London: The Social Scene of Early Modernism*, 2004.

A bohemian woman could be a *grisette*, mistress, muse, model, wife-mother, salon hostess, independent woman, worker, free spirit, lesbian or artist. Euphemia adopted several roles, and the reward was the freedom to be a sexual adventuress and a muse. Euphemia used her seductive powers to attract interesting and creative men and women, and to advance herself and acquire power. She created a magic and a mystery which could be destructive but also incredibly creative. Euphemia was a cultural enabler and co-created several great works of art and literature. This is her story, and the story of her lovers and of the art and literature that she inspired from 1905 to 1915.

ONE

Manchester 1905

She is sweet, with her amazed child's eyes,
with her blonde braids pulled up above each ear.
Everyone looks at her everywhere. – Henri-Pierre Roché

ON A STREET IN MANCHESTER a girl noticed a boy and decided to follow him. Her curiosity that day changed her life and his, forever. Nina Forrest, a seventeen-year-old working-class girl, pursued a medical student she saw leaving the Manchester Infirmary. She followed him through Rusholme to the Manchester City Art School. Henry Lamb was aware of his pursuer but played along and on reaching his destination, turned and confronted her. Dumbfounded by what he saw, the apparition of a Viking Madonna, he assumed she must have come to model at the art school and invited her in. Dissimulation being one of Nina's great talents, she agreed that she was indeed an artist's model. He ushered her to his studio where he began to draw the perfect symmetry of her face.

Henry was a disgruntled medical student who dreamed of becoming an artist. He was impressed with this new model's ability to change her pose on request and as he sat and sketched her, he could not fail to observe and record her corn-blonde lustrous hair, her pale milky skin, her cornflower blue eyes, her full-lipped sensual mouth, all set within an oval face reminiscent of a Mantegna saint. Her long, muscular limbs and the easy facility with which she moved her body enthralled him. She had a great sense of theatre and comedy and entertained him with her irreverent stories. The attraction went both ways. Nina found Henry to be almost as beautiful as a girl, with fine, delicate features and penetrating eyes. No one had ever observed her so intently before; he fixed her with his eyes and then looked at his paper, he asked her to keep her eyes downturned. Nina realised that for them to continue their flirtation she would need to conceal her working-class background. For now, like Hardy's Tess, her beauty trumped considerations of birth and breeding and Henry was smitten.

We don't know how Henry and Nina first met; the above is an imagined scenario which takes into account their close geographical proximity to one another, the fact that Nina may well have been invited to be an artist's model and my suggestion that she may have been an agent in making it happen given her guile. It was a narcissistic twinning; beautiful girl meets beautiful boy. Both parties were dissatisfied with their lives in Manchester. Nina wanted to escape poverty and a difficult family life; she wanted more than a future as a shopgirl or a mill worker. Similarly, Henry was suffocated by a snobbish and Edwardian academic family who dismissed his dreams of becoming an artist. Although they had encouraged his artistic and cultural education at Manchester Grammar School (he was an accomplished musician and his father Horace, the Professor of Mathematics at the University of Manchester, had taken him on an art tour of Italy) the expectation was that Henry would qualify as a medical doctor and settle down to a respectable professional life. However, both Nina and Henry wanted something quite different for their lives than their circumstances currently suggested. The conversation during the sitting had interested her enormously; Henry was full of ideas and spoke of books he had read and his passion for art. Nina was immediately attracted to his mind. Their meeting led to a romantic spark but also provided the opportunity for another sort of collaboration; a creative one.

When Henry showed Nina the pencil sketch of her head, she experienced the thrill of being seen in a completely new way. This young man had captured her like a fly in amber for posterity. It was a revelation. She saw another version of herself reflected at her, lovely and pure and without the pain and degradation of her actual life. She was exhilarated. It was difficult for her to disentangle the romantic feelings from the feelings of empowerment and opportunity. Nina was aware that she was attractive to the opposite sex, but this was a more potent feeling. This young man had immortalised her on paper. Henry was also pleased with the drawing and what this young girl had

Henry Lamb, *Nina*, pencil on paper, 1905

unleashed in him artistically. The creative union enhanced the romantic feelings, and they saw in each other the opportunity to escape their lives in dreary Manchester.

In 1905, Manchester was still a city of dark Satanic mills and belching chimneys. It was a maze of black soot-covered brick houses, row after row of tenements and narrow alleyways, interrupted only by factories, textile mills, dying works, gasometers and chemical plants. The air was thick with smoke. Nature was only to be found along the canals that criss-crossed the city and in parks that surrounded large houses, such as the Lamb family home on Wilbraham Road in Fallowfield.

Henry Lamb, *Young Self Portrait with Fedora,* etching, 1906

Henry found the Manchester of his childhood sordid and ugly and longed to escape. Nina's small tenement was in a crowded slum not far from Henry's family home geographically, but socially there was a huge chasm. Nina was secretive and never introduced Henry to her family. She was able to disguise her Mancunian accent; her parents were Scottish, and she chose to affect a neutral voice.

Nina lived with her mother, stepfather and siblings. In later years, rumours circulated that Nina's mother had been a prostitute. There is no evidence for this, but Henry Lamb did describe Nina being on friendly terms with a group of women who sat in their dressing gowns outside their front doors in the red-light district. He was aware of her lowly origins.

Although Henry was bored with his own family and yearned to escape from their respectable Edwardian clutches, he did introduce Nina to his mother. Her beauty and personality must have been sufficient to disguise her lack of education and class. Henry was a diligent medical student. Despite abandoning his medical studies in 1905, at the outbreak of the First World War he returned to them and qualified as a doctor. He saw active service as the medical officer of the 5th Battalion, Royal Inniskilling Fusiliers and was awarded the Military Cross. He yearned to be an artist and, having been encouraged by his art teacher at school, while at university attended classes at the Manchester City Art School where he became friends with the artists Francis Dodd and Bernard Leach.

The meeting of Nina and Henry catalysed something in both; their ambition for another life and the possibility of escape. They made an excellent team and unleashed something in each other which would propel them into a more transgressive lifestyle. In the few weeks of their courtship, the relationship had rapidly progressed, and the couple had decided in June 1905 to elope to London. Henry was convinced that if only he could get to London, he could become an artist. His hero Augustus John had just opened an art school in Chelsea, with the Irish artist William Orpen. Henry could enrol there. In the meantime, his mentor Francis Dodd had moved to London and could help him; his friend Bernard Leach was also in London. Henry's older brother Walter Lamb was studying at the University of Cambridge and there had made friends with Thoby Stephen and Clive Bell; he could introduce Henry to a group of young intellectuals who were interested in art and literature, living a less constrained and more bohemian life in London.

TWO

London 1905–06 Bloomsbury and Chelsea

She is 17 years old, snowy flesh,
periwinkle eyes, long blonde hair,
a rich, fresh pink mouth. – Henri-Pierre Roché

THE ELOPEMENT WAS SCANDALOUS. But Nina and Henry were lovestruck and carefree. Nina's lowly social origins meant that she had little to lose; she was much less bound to social propriety than a middle-class girl would have been. Nina had no prospects in Manchester apart from menial work and marriage. Henry and the plan to go to London must have seemed like a wonderful opportunity. She was galvanised by his talent and knew that if the worst happened, he would still have his respectable family to fall back on. Henry had a safety net, and she was prepared to take a risk. She had been friendly with the prostitutes in Manchester, so the fall from grace would have been an imaginable and ordinary risk to Nina – she wanted adventure and excitement.

They arrived in London and found separate lodgings. Henry immediately went to visit Francis Dodd who lived in Chiswick. They also visited the artist Muirhead Bone (married to Dodd's sister) who lived in Chiswick Mall which Nina thought was beautiful, with large Georgian houses and villas nestled on the banks of the river Thames. Like Dickens as a boy seeing the mansion at Gad's Hill, Nina made a mental note that if ever fortune were to come her way, this was the place she would like to live.

Bernard Leach was working for a London bank and met the young ingénues; he later said that he didn't know how they existed as they had no money. He helped them find lodgings in Paultons Square in Chelsea. Henry Lamb sat for a portrait for Francis Dodd and as soon as the Chelsea Art School opened, he enrolled. Augustus John, already an artist of some repute, was delighted by his new acolyte, Henry, and equally by

Augustus John, *Portrait of Henry Lamb (1885–1960) c. 1908* pencil on paper, 25.4 x 20.3 cm

his girlfriend and model, Nina. Nina was put to work immediately as an artist's model at the Chelsea Art School, modelling for Henry and other students, including Edna Clarke Hall and Maresco Pearce.

Whilst Henry was busy in his studio, there was the problem of what Nina would do if she were not modelling. Walter Lamb introduced the runaways to his Cambridge friend Thoby Stephen, who thought that his sisters might be able to keep Nina entertained. His sisters were Vanessa, later to become Vanessa Bell, the painter, and Virginia Woolf, the novelist and essayist. In 1905 the two girls had recently moved to 46 Gordon Square, Bloomsbury with their brothers Thoby and Adrian Stephen, and were living life in considerably more freedom after the death of their parents. Vanessa wanted to be an artist and was eager to meet Henry Lamb. Virginia was recently recovering from a period of poor mental health. Their correspondence from this period suggests that the whole Stephen family was delighted by the arrival of Henry Lamb and Miss Forrest.

In their new Bloomsbury address, Vanessa and Virginia were keen to throw over the Victorian strictures and censoriousness of their parents and live independently in a modern way. Virginia wrote:

'In October 1904, 46 Gordon Square was the most beautiful, the most exciting, the most romantic place in the world. To begin with it was astonishing to stand at the drawing room window and look into all those trees. Here Vanessa and I each had a sitting room; there was a large double drawing room; and a study on the ground floor. Instead of Morris wallpapers we decorated our walls with washes of plain distemper. We were full of experiments and reforms. We were going to do without table-napkins, we were going to have large supplies of Bromo[1] instead; we were going to paint; to write; to have coffee after dinner instead of tea at 9 o'clock. Everything was going to be new; everything was going to be different, everything was on trial... Bloomsbury is ever so much more interesting than Kensington – visiting a picture gallery and coming home to find the drawing room full of the oddest collections of people.'[2]

Into this drawing room and social experiment in June 1905 walked Nina Forrest and Henry Lamb. They decided that Nina would have to come up with an explanation for her obscure origins and her

1. Bromo was an antacid cure.
2. Virginia Woolf, 'Old Bloomsbury', *Moments of Being*, 1920.

Henry Lamb, *Euphemia Lamb*, 1906, pencil on paper, 29.8 x 23.5 cm

elopement with Henry that would satisfy the Stephen family and their albeit modern, Edwardian social mores. Vanessa was clearly delighted with Henry Lamb and accepted his request that she help his friend Miss Forrest. Vanessa and Henry met in a teashop in the King's Road in December 1905 to discuss the possibility of sharing a studio. Vanessa wrote:

Photographs of Vanessa Stephens (left) and her sister, Virginia (right), 1902

'Lamb in his corduroys, smoking a pipe… and I thought with joy how shocked all my friends and relations would be if they could only come in and see us! But our conversation was most innocent and all about Miss Forrest.'[3]

In a letter to her friend Margery Snowden, Vanessa described the plight of Miss Forrest:

'Her family wanted her to marry a Russian Count. They forced her to get engaged to him and he wanted to marry her. Whilst engaged to him she met Mr. Lamb in Manchester. He was then a medical student & very clever and she told me, very affected. She didn't like him at first in consequence but she then made friends with him & I suppose he was about the first intelligent person she had got to know. She told him or he knew about the Russian.

3. Vanessa Bell, letter to Margery Snowden, 1905, Tate Archives.

Anyhow she asked him to help her for she had not the courage to escape the man herself. He said it was wrong for her to marry without love & saw the Russian and seems to have talked him into giving her up. Then they both came to London – he to lodgings as an artist & she to other lodgings with no idea at all of what people would think.

I wished very much I could help her for I like her & I think her ignorance makes her position very hard upon her. She is not the least flirtatious, but perfectly simple & open, coming out occasionally with regular terrible infant remarks and not in the least seeing why they should shock.'

A few days later Vanessa updated Margery on the Miss Forrest situation:

'All our talk was about her unfortunate circumstances. He [Henry Lamb] quite sees how difficult the position is & I think feels responsible for her but you can understand that a boy of 22 or thereabouts knowing hardly anyone in London doesn't know what to do at all. We settled in the end that I should try & find some place where she could live & some work of a practical kind that she could do. Of course, a place like A.H.[4] would be no good for she is not a student. But I think I can probably find some other place of the same kind only not so big. She has plenty of money so there might not be much difficulty – the only thing is that she may be persuaded to go there & stay there and work regularly, but I think she might do and it would be the best thing possible for her whether she married Lamb eventually or not.

I don't yet call her Nina though she has asked me to, but I soon shall! & do you think there is any harm in it? After all what should we ever do if we stopped to consider the possible harmful results? In this case I really have no fears –

---

4. Ames House, a women's hostel in Mortimer Street, Soho built by the YWCA in 1904.

for one thing I don't believe that Lamb and Nina are in love with each other.'[5]

Vanessa Stephen was keen to further her acquaintance with them and was intrigued by their elopement. One senses some disapproval of Nina's situation but nevertheless she was taken in and help was offered. There was talk of her and Henry sharing an art studio at one point but this came to nothing. Nina had told Vanessa a made-up version of her history:

> 'She told me a good deal of her history rather incoherently, but I came in the end to a fairly clear idea of her most extraordinary past existence. It's too full of ins and outs to be repeated at length and it sounds like a medieval romance – but I believe it's true.
>
> 'She seems to have been deserted by her family and hardly ever to have lived with them. They are quite rich, and they alternately neglect her entirely & have her to live with them for short intervals when they spoil her. She seems to have had no education and to have lived with some very second-rate people going about from one house to another and being adopted by various friends and relations in turn.'[6]

Nina had embroidered her origin story with great enthusiasm. This was believed by the Stephen family at the time, adding to her mystery and their fascination with her.

Lytton Strachey, the writer and friend of the Stephen family, also met Henry and Nina in December 1905.

Lytton Strachey was very taken with Henry Lamb. He met him soon after his arrival in London and wrote to Leonard Woolf (in Ceylon) in December 1905, that Lamb had:

> '... run away from Manchester, become an artist, grown side whiskers. I didn't speak to him but I wanted to, because he

---

5. Vanessa Bell, letter to Margery Snowden, 1905, Tate Archives.
6. Ibid.

looked really amazing, though of course very, very bad.'

Lytton was a homosexual and fell in love with Lamb. He was less impressed with Nina. He described her to Leonard Woolf as:

'… Lamb's quasi mistress, a very young woman dressed in the regulation harlot clothes.'

Adrian Stephen was in love with both Henry and Nina. Walter Lamb writes:

'[Adrian] thinks Henry beautiful, as well as his fiancée, and he announced his intention of being a regular visitor to his garret in Chelsea.'

Lytton Strachey informs us that:

'Adrian and Henry Lamb had been spending a week in an Inn in the New Forest. It's supposed that Adrian is in love with HL and I shouldn't be surprised if he were – the face is so astoundingly attractive. I talked to HL about his exploits with Adrian and he described their daily life – their walking, hunting etc. I couldn't help saying at the end "And how did you spend your evenings?" But HL was discreet.'[7]

What was Nina doing during the week Henry spent with Adrian? She was thrown upon Adrian's sisters, Vanessa and Virginia.

What did Virginia Stephen make of Miss Forrest? She had mixed feelings. She wrote to her great friend Violet Dickinson:

'We have been landed with Miss Forrest… She sits vaguely in the drawing room for hours and forgets whether she had tea or dinner last, whether children have meat or wine. My head

---

7. Lytton Strachey, letter to Leonard Woolf, 9 January 1906, Berg Collection, New York.

Henry Lamb, *Portrait of Euphemia Lamb*, *c.* 1906, pencil on paper, 23.5 x 20.9 cm

spins with her stories; until I say sternly "Miss Forrest take my advice and learn Greek". It is like a nightmare.'[8]

Virginia was less gullible than her sister when it came to Nina's wild stories and fabrications about her life but, nevertheless, she was interested in her.

Nina did make a lasting impression on Virginia, and she appeared in Virginia's letters and diaries for many years. There are striking

8. Virginia Woolf, letter to Violet Dickinson, 3 January 1906, from *The Letters of Virginia Woolf 1888–1912*, Vol. 1, ed. by N. Nicolson, p. 215.

similarities between Virginia's descriptions of Miss Forrest and her later creation of the character Florinda, the distant and unreliable young woman with whom Jacob Flanders falls in love, in her 1922 novel *Jacob's Room*:

'As for Florinda's story, her name had been bestowed upon her by a painter who had wished to signify that the flower of her maidenhood was still unplucked. Be that as it may, she was without a surname, and for parents had only a photograph of a tombstone beneath which she said her father was buried. Sometimes she would dwell on the size of it, and rumour had it that Florinda's father had died from the growth of his bones which nothing could stop; just as her mother enjoyed the confidence of the Royal Master, and now and again Florinda was a Princess, but chiefly when drunk. Thus deserted, pretty into the bargain, with tragic eyes and the lips of a child, she talked more about virginity than women mostly do, and had lost it only the night before, or cherished it beyond the heart in her breast, according to the man she talked to.'

Nina later became known as Euphemia. Henry decided to call her Euphemia, her middle name, as it added to her mystery and concealed her origins. She had regaled Virginia and Vanessa with far-fetched and inconsistent tall stories about her background. She was exceptionally pretty, with full lips, and of questionable morals. She spent weeks sitting with the Stephen sisters at Gordon Square; Vanessa painted her, and it is highly likely that she entered Virginia's imaginative life too. *Jacob's Room* is an experimental novel and a portrait of a young man who is both representative and victim of the social values which led Edwardian society into war. The novel traces Jacob's life as a small boy playing on a beach, his years in Cambridge, then in artistic London, followed by a trip to Greece and then his untimely death in the war. Virginia used the template of her brother Thoby's life for the study of Jacob. We know that Thoby invited Lytton to Gordon Square on 26 January 1906, the only other guests being the Lambs:

Augustus John, *Euphemia*, pencil on paper, 36.2 x 23 cm

'Jacob took her word for it that she was chaste. She prattled sitting by the fireside of famous painters. The tomb of her father was mentioned. Wild and frail and beautiful, she looked, and thus the women of the Greeks were, Jacob thought: and thus was life; and himself a man and Florinda chaste. She left with one of Shelley's poems beneath her arm. Mrs Stuart (her landlady) often talked of him. Marvellous are the innocent. To believe that the girl herself transcends all lies (for Jacob was not such a fool as to believe implicitly), to wonder enviously at the unattached life – his own seeming potted and even cloistered in comparison – to have at hand as sovereign species for all disorders of the soul Adonais and the plays of Shakespeare; to figure out a comradeship all but equal on both, for women, thought Jacob, are just the same as men – innocence such as this is marvellous enough and perhaps not so foolish after all.'

Virginia's commentary on the freedom of Florinda chimes with comments she wrote about Nina in her diary in 1920, whilst she would have been writing *Jacob's Room*:

'I see her as someone in mid ocean, struggling, diving, while I pace the bank.'[9]

As the novel progresses, the characterisation of Florinda becomes more vicious and is written without much compassion. Woolf is commenting on how a man like Jacob cannot resist the appeal of Florinda's sexuality, but also how it stirs up in him a violent revulsion:

'The problem is insoluble. The body is harnessed to a brain. Beauty goes hand in hand with stupidity. There she sat staring at the fire as she had stared at the broken mustard pot. In spite of defending indecency, Jacob doubted whether he liked it in the raw. He had a violent reversion towards male society,

9. Virginia Woolf, diary, 2 August 1920, *The Diary of Virginia Woolf: 1920–24*, Vol. 2, p. 66.

cloistered rooms and the works of the classics; and was ready to turn with wrath upon whoever it was who had fashioned life thus. Then Florinda laid her hand upon his knee. After all it was none of her fault. But the thought saddened him… But when she looked at him, dumbly, half guessing, half understanding, apologising… straight and beautiful in body, her face like a shell within its cap, then he knew that cloisters and classics are no use whatever. The problem is insoluble.'

In *Jacob's Room*, Woolf writes a wonderfully experimental sex scene between Jacob and Florinda from the perspective of an unopened letter lying on the hall table outside the bedroom. In an Oedipal twist, the letter is from Jacob's mother and can see and hear the goings-on of the young couple.

Woolf was commenting on the inequality in power between men and women by lambasting Florinda as a brainless character who nevertheless overpowers Jacob's thoughts and intellectual ideals. Florinda may have been brainless, but Nina was not. Living in close proximity with this highly intellectual group of individuals would have made Nina aware of her own lack of education, but she would also have discovered that she too had a mind and intelligence enough to keep up. Virginia Woolf has Florinda carrying around a copy of Shelley, but according to Vanessa the Stephen family was being encouraged by Clive Bell to read the novel *Dangerous Liaisons* by Pierre Choderlos de Laclos, and it is likely that Euphemia would have read it too.

THREE

Wild and Frail
and Beautiful

She is a beggar or a princess, we don't know.
– Henri-Pierre Roché

VANESSA BELL AND HENRY LAMB were founding members of the Friday Club. The first exhibition, which opened in October 1905, comprised works by them. There were also Friday Club meetings where the artists discussed art, and we know that Nina hid behind a curtain until her presence was discovered at one of these early meetings.

Lytton Strachey wrote to Leonard Woolf in February 1906:

'I forgot to give an account of the Friday Club. It was in Henry Lamb's studio in Chelsea – a large square room, with a great north sloping window. There was a vast collection of persons – nearly all artists, or quasi artists, male and female. The whole Gothic [Stephen] family was of course there, and I came with Pippa [sister] and Duncan. [Desmond] MacCarthy had not naturally written a paper, so he spoke it as best he might. It was the vaguest maunder about "art" and "technique" and "surface" and "the beauty of what was represented", but it served the purpose of rousing a rowdy discussion.'

During the summer of 1905 Henry turned to Francis Dodd, his mentor from Manchester. Francis was established in London and a member of the New English Art Club. Lamb's portrait of Nina was accepted and exhibited at the New English Art Club in October 1905. It was an astonishing success for the ingénue Lamb and it also heralded Nina's arrival onto the English art scene as a model.

Henry and Nina's risky plan to move to London looked as

Augustus John, *Portrait of Euphemia Lamb*, *c.* 1908, pencil on paper

though it was paying dividends. Henry had had a drawing accepted by the New English Art Club and he had formed the Friday Club with Vanessa Stephen, Clive Bell and others. He had made the acquaintance of Augustus John and enrolled at his Chelsea Art School. Nina had been accepted into London bohemian society without too much trouble. Nina found herself in a new and alien world, where art and books and ideas were valued and taken seriously; her immersion into

Francis Dodd, *Henry Lamb*, 1905, oil on canvas, 71.7 x 53.2 cm

bohemian culture was rapid. Her role as an artist's model would have given her ample opportunity to hear different artists' discourse on their work and life in general. It was an education for Nina and her mind devoured the new knowledge and ideas. Nina was funny, irreverent and surprisingly (to herself and to others) intelligent.

Nina and Henry would have met a wide variety of artists, writers and thinkers during their first stay in London. Virginia Woolf wrote about the collection of persons one could have expected to find in their 46 Gordon Square drawing room:

'There was Augustus John, very sinister in a black stock and a velvet coat, Winston Churchill, very rubicund, all gold lace and medals, on his way to Buckingham Palace; Raymond Asquith crackling with epigrams; Francis Dodd telling me most graphically how he and Aunt Susie had killed bugs. There was Lord Henry Bentinck at one end of the sofa and perhaps Nina Lamb at the other. There was Philip Morrell, there was Gilbert Cannan, there was Bertie Russell, above all there was Ottoline herself.'[1]

Henry Lamb came under the influence of Augustus John – he had moved to London purposely to study under the famous artist. Bernard Leach recalled the first meeting between Henry and Augustus at the Chelsea Art School:

'Augustus came in late straight from some party looking well-groomed and remarkably handsome, picked up a drawing board, and instead of using it, sat behind this new student and watched him for half an hour. They talked and Augustus invited Henry to his home.'[2]

Their relationship blossomed and Henry felt more at home with Augustus John, both artistically and temperamentally in terms of his bohemian ways. John was a genuine inspiration. He was a Welsh artist who had been known at the Slade as the best draughtsman of his generation.

Photograph of Augustus John, 1902

1. Virginia Woolf, 'Old Bloomsbury', *Moments of Being*, 1920, pp. 216–17.
2. Leach, *Beyond East and West*, pp. 31–2.

In the first decade of the twentieth century, he was becoming one of the most important artists at work in Britain. Virginia Woolf remarked that by 1908 'the era of John Singer Sargent was over, and the age of Augustus John was dawning.'

Henry Lamb's arrival on the English art scene of this period caused quite a stir. He was seen to have outstanding potential as an artist. Maresco Pearce, a fellow artist who met Henry during his time at the Chelsea Art school, described him thus:

> 'I met him at the Chelsea School and was enormously impressed – less by his brilliant & really beautiful drawing than by his even more brilliant intelligence – a rather cold, aloof intelligence & never felt particularly intimate with him, but being in the same studio with him for days & he is a great talker & a good listener, constituted a certain sort of intimacy.'

Pearce recalled Lamb reading Otto Weininger's book *Sex and Character: An Investigation of Fundamental Principles.* The substance of his argument in the book is that emancipation is only possible for a masculine woman – and that the female life is consumed with the sexual function, both the act (for example as a prostitute) and the product (for example as a mother). By contrast, the duty of the male, or the masculine aspect of the personality, is to strive to become a genius and to forgo sexuality. A significant part of the book is about the nature of genius. Weininger shot himself (in the house where Beethoven had died) aged twenty-three. Nina would have been absorbing these new and novel ideas about gender.

Henry and Nina visited Paris early in 1906. Nina may have become pregnant on this trip. On their return they married

Photograph of Henry Lamb, 1910s

Augustus John, *Portrait of Euphemia Lamb*, 1906

on 10 May 1906 at Chelsea Registry Office with Augustus John and Walter Lamb as witnesses. There was no baby, so there may have been a miscarriage, an illegal operation or Nina may have pretended to be pregnant to gain greater security. Nina Forrest became Nina Lamb. They had a honeymoon in Wiltshire and soon after returned to London. Walter Lamb wrote to his friend Clive Bell in London:

> 'I should be glad if you could renew your acquaintance with my brother Harry, who has set himself up as an artist at 125 Cheyne Walk, Chelsea. I daresay he feels a little lonely… I know he is on the lookout for any job which will put something into his pockets.'

Virginia Stephen recalled in May 1906:

'Lamb and Nina have finally drifted into marriage. At the
Friday Club last week, we sat and listened to this kind of
thing… "Well Nina. Are you married?" Nina: "Oh no, I'm not
married. That is I am married. I think I was married yesterday,
and I was so hungry the whole time, and I had a new blouse,
and a cake."[3]

Virginia described Henry and Nina as a 'stunted kind of nightmare'
and claimed to be unable even to take a 'psychological interest in them'.
Nevertheless, she remained fascinated by them. Virginia caricatured
Nina's scatty, vague and whimsical nature. Given what we know about
Bloomsbury's socially transgressive mores, it suggests that Henry and
Nina shocked their Edwardian sensibilities. Keith Clements in his
biography of Henry Lamb argued that it was Nina's amorous adventures
that so intrigued Virginia, that she may have seen in Nina a fascinating
reflection of another self, the possibility of an extrovert and passionate
alter ego to reverse the containment of her own private life. Their
elopement, their sex life, the abortion, were all new and uncomfortable
ideas for the embryonic Bloomsburies to absorb.

Shortly after her marriage to Henry, Nina agreed to sit for a
painting by Vanessa. Vanessa was being courted by Clive Bell and was
considering his second proposal of marriage. In 1906, shortly before
their engagement, she wrote a frank and intimate letter to Clive about
her painting of Nina:

'You would have found me with Nina. She came at 1.30 having
already had lunch. Vaguely imagining we had ours about 12.
So I had mine in a hurry and painted her until 4. Listening at
the same time to appallingly sordid histories of her love affairs.
She is known in Paris as a – could it be a "Lesbian!" Although
Sapphist will do as well and then she told me awful secret tales

3. Virginia Woolf, letter to Violet Dickinson, May 1906, from *The Letters of Virginia Woolf 1888–1912*,
Vol. 1, ed. by N. Nicolson, p. 219.

Photograph of Vanessa Stephen (Bell) painting *Portrait of Lady Robert Cecil*, 1905, from life, at Gordon Square

of how Henry Lamb performed an illegal operation upon her!

It sounds too grotesque. In the midst of all this the bell rang, and I awaited Gwenny [Raverat] for I had told her I would be at home today. I thought of Darwin niceness confronted by Nina – but to my surprise in walked Lytton. Nina went at once after tea to my relief for I thought Lytton would be too much disgusted.'[4]

4. Vanessa Bell, letter to Clive Bell, 1906, Tate Archives 8010.2.21.

Henry Lamb, *Head of a Girl*, *c.* 1907, charcoal on paper, 22.5 x 24 cm

The Bloomsbury Group is today famous for its rejection of bourgeois habits and the conventions of Victorian life and its new focus on personal relationships and individual pleasure. But the contemporary accounts of Virginia, Vanessa and Lytton's reactions to Nina and Henry suggest the Stephen family was shocked by the runaway couple's unconventional lives. These new attitudes towards sexuality and women were later adopted by the Bloomsbury Group. In 1922, Virginia Woolf wrote her reminiscences of Old Bloomsbury:

'I should be sorry to tell you how old I was before I saw that there is nothing shocking in a man's having a mistress, or in a woman's being one.'[5]

Henry and Nina were important early influences in their new ways of living and conducting oneself both socially and sexually. As time went on, they gravitated away from Vanessa and Virginia and were drawn more into the very bohemian circle of Augustus John. But the Bloomsbury connection was maintained because when Henry and Nina moved to Paris, they lived in the same street as Duncan Grant and became embroiled in his affairs of the heart.

5. Virginia Woolf, 'Old Bloomsbury', *Moments of Being*, 1920, p. 212–13.

FOUR

Paris 1907–08

*She went to the Luxembourg Gardens
and threw her diabolo higher than all the others.*
– Henri-Pierre Roché

HENRY AND NINA LAMB arrived in Paris in February of 1907 at the invitation of Augustus John. In fact, it was John's wife Ida's idea to invite them to Paris with the idea that John could use Nina as a model; she wrote to a friend that it would be nice to have 'Lambs on the doorstep'. Augustus John, the talented and established painter, had already installed Ida and his mistress Dorelia in Paris with his children. The ménage à trois had worked well initially, with the two women living together and raising John's children. They seemed to get along with each other better in John's absence. There was even a rumour that the two women might have become lovers. However, around this time Dorelia and her child moved out to another apartment. Meanwhile, in London John had taken another lover, Alick Schepeler. Henry and Nina took an apartment in rue Cels in Montparnasse, near Dorelia's new place. Ida wrote to a close friend that the Lambs were 'both delightful' and described Nina as:

'A beauty of seventeen with grey corn coloured hair'.

Augustus was hopeful that Henry's presence would help the family dynamics, since Dorelia and he had got on very well, both were musical and liked to play the piano. At first everything went well. Henry began to dress like John and adopted the bohemian garb of neckerchief, corduroy jacket and earrings and a beard. He admired John as an artist and for his superb skills as a draughtsman, but he also wanted to emulate him as a bohemian and imitate his gypsy appearance. Although John was

Augustus John, *Portrait of a Woman*, pencil on paper

Augustus John, *The Way Down to the Sea*, 1909, oil on canvas, 76 × 67 cm

the more famous artist, he appreciated Lamb's encouragement. He told Dorelia that Lamb 'wants to be my apprentice' and that he was grateful that Lamb had such faith in him as an artist.

There is an incident from this time involving Augustus John teaching Nina to ride a bicycle:

> 'Nina, lovely and ash blonde, in black velvet, a yellow scarlet muffler and a great display of black silk stocking, curvetted and staggered down the road, with John, in corduroy trousers, jersey, golden ear-rings, and carrot beard and hair, dashing after her.'[1]

---

1. C.R.W. Nevinson, *Paint and Prejudice*, p. 47.

There were some dissenting voices, notably Percy Wyndham Lewis. Lewis wrote to his mother:

> 'John has a very disagreeable set of people round him just now, and the average morality, taste, sensibility, or whatever one calls it of the average English medical student who has read Nietzsche prevails among these persons.'

Montparnasse was a neighbourhood with wide streets and large cafés, at the intersection of the boulevard du Montparnasse and the boulevard Raspail. Rents were cheap and artists and writers flocked there, having seen Paris with its rich history of Baudelaire, Rimbaud and Verlaine as the centre of the avant-garde since the 1850s. The concentration of creative talent enabled experimental writing, art, music and dance to flourish there. The cafés became the places where artists met, writers gathered and models like Nina looked for work. There was a crop of new art academies in the area and Henry decided to enrol in La Palette.

Duncan Grant wrote to his cousin Lytton in February:

> 'Friday night, Mon Dieu, Walter's brother Henry has turned up here! And what do you ever think is living in the same street cum concubine?'

In fact, Duncan was also studying painting at La Palette and living in the rue des Cels. Henry and Nina would have known Duncan from his attendance at the Friday Club in London.

Duncan described his average day at La Palette in his memoirs:

> 'Every morning I found it an effort to wake up, have my coffee & brioche at a nearby creamerie and be at La Palette by 8 o'clock. The morning's work was finished at 12 noon. By that time I was very hungry and turned to a little restaurant (name forgotten) in the blvd St Germain. It rhymed with Thackery and was mainly patronised by students (cost about 7 francs with coffee). I spent most of the afternoon at the Louvre,

Blanche would take his students on a Monday when it was closed and talk about a picture we would copy. I found him a stimulating and exciting Professor. My favourite meal was potato soup and confiture d'orange. Evenings I might study drawings in the library of the Beaux Arts.'

A few weeks after the arrival of Henry and Nina everything was thrown into chaos. Ida John was expecting her fifth child and we know that the night before she went into childbirth, Henry Lamb took her out to a music hall. Ida delivered her fifth child, another son, but then developed puerperal fever.

Duncan Grant writing of events in his memoirs of his time in Paris:

'Then there was the formidable Augustus John and with Dorelia and Dorelia's sister all living in a whitewashed shelter near the Lion de Beffort. John's first wife was dying in childbirth in hospital.'

Ida died on 14 March 1907. Her mother arranged her cremation at the Père-Lachaise cemetery and Henry Lamb organised a memorial for friends and family. Ambrose McEvoy arrived from London but got so drunk he missed his ferry home. Nina helped Dorelia and her sister Edie look after the children.

Vanessa Bell, who was in Paris at this time on her honeymoon, wrote to her friend Margery Snowden:

'Nina has charge of two of John's children.'

In his grief John went on a drunken spree.
Wyndham Lewis wrote to his mother about Ida's death and added:

'John has been drunk for the last three days so I can't tell you if he is pleased or sorry. I think he's sorry though.'

In the aftermath of this tragic event, things unravelled in Henry

Henry Lamb, *Self Portrait*, 1905, pencil on paper

and Nina's volatile relationship. They had never been temperamentally suited, with both of them stubborn and quick to bouts of temper. However, it was clear that during their time in Paris, Henry had been falling in love with Dorelia. The chaos following Ida's death brought them into more intimate contact with each other, and they declared their feelings for one another. This was a double blow for Nina, as she was good friends with Dorelia too, and to have been betrayed by both her best friend and her husband was devastating.

Augustus John, *Euphemia Head*, *c.* 1908, pencil on paper

Soon afterwards, Henry and Dorelia left Paris together and consummated their relationship. Nina had been completely reliant on Henry and this was a terrible blow. She could have gone home back to Manchester with her tail between her legs, but she did not. She decided to use her social capital and her charms, and fell into the arms of their friend and neighbour, Duncan Grant.

In March 1907, Duncan Grant wrote to Lytton Strachey:

'Oh! I never told you that I spend a great many of my evenings in a young lady's bedroom. No it is no good you making a face.'

Lytton responded:

'No! You won't get a rise out of me about your "young lady" and her "bedroom". Ho ho!'

By April 1907, Duncan provided more details:

'And then that Lamb family sickens me and the painter John I'm convinced now he's a bad lot. His mistress Dorelia fell in love with Henry and invited him to copulate and as far as I can see John encouraged the liaison and arranged at any rate to keep Nina out of the way. Although Henry didn't in the least want to have any dealings with Dorelia. However it was apparently all fixed up that they should "go on the roads together" when Nina was according to her own story, found with a loaded revolver ready to shoot herself (as far as I can gather). So Henry has left by himself and is now who knows where with a huge Knapsack on his back trudging towards Italy. Dorelia and John seem to be the devils and the others merely absurd. But Nina seems somehow to have lurched on to me. Isn't it all sickening & silly? For God's sake don't let Walter know or anyone because I suppose the less that those respectable old things know the better. Meanwhile I have been dining occasionally with Bell & Vanessa, Adrian & Virginia. What a quartet. I seem to like them all so much, after these fops and fights.'

Lytton responded:

'I draw a line, because I want to separate off the horrible Lamb ménage from other things. Keynes gave me a vague sketch of the business, and I immediately had just the feelings you describe. Sickening and silly is all that can be said of it. I'm sorry you've come up against it, and as for Nina hanging onto you, it really is depressing, but I'm sure the whole filthy

Alvin Langdon Coburn, photograph of Duncan Grant *c.* 1912

business will pass away from you. But John! Oh lawks! What a "warning" as the Clergy say. When I think of him, I often feel that the only thing to do is to chuck up everything and make a dash for some such safe secluded office-stool as is pressed by Maynard's bottom. The dangers of freedom are appalling!'

Nina's relationship with Duncan Grant was short-lived but he provided a shoulder to cry on and some compassion and support whilst she worked out what to do. Nina and Henry did not divorce until the late 1920s, but she took this set-back as an opportunity to reinvent herself as a new woman with a new name. From now on she became Euphemia Lamb. Euphemia was her middle name and there is a sense that she took this opportunity to create herself as a café cocotte and artist's model, not just a wife. By now she had friends, work as a model and a smattering of the French language but more importantly, she had a sense of herself as a beautiful, sexual, charismatic and intelligent woman with lots of opportunities. Euphemia would have seen at first hand, with Ida and Dorelia and their seven children, how easy it was for the bohemian lifestyle to destroy the lives of the women who were handservants to their successful artist husbands, and how the supposedly unconventional lifestyle ended up with the same drudgery of domesticity that she had been seeking to escape.

Euphemia had been actively helping Ida and Dorelia with their children; she saw how these women had sacrificed their artistic careers and, in Ida's case, regretted it. In the dark days after Ida's death, Augustus' sister, Gwen John, came to help with the children too, so Euphemia would have met her. Gwen was Rodin's muse and lover during this period, but she was also painting and was determined to become an artist on her own terms. Gwen had vowed never to marry nor procreate because in that she saw the death of her artistic potential and power. Rainer Maria Rilke, the Austro–German poet, was working as Rodin's secretary during this period and was a friend of Gwen's. Gwen took heed of Rilke's advice that the life of an artist should be one of great interiority. It is a striking fact that despite many amorous adventures and pregnancy scares, Euphemia did not have a baby until 1915.

FIVE

Paris – The Dangers of Freedom are Appalling

She is exquisite, men desire her.
– Henri-Pierre Roché

WHAT DID EUPHEMIA DO NEXT? With Henry off on his walk towards Italy, she had time alone. She amused herself with Duncan for a couple of weeks.

In April 1907, Lytton wrote to Duncan:

'What is Paris looking like and whether Nina still obsesses you?'

Lytton also wrote to Leonard Woolf, who was overseas, with the gossip:

'But I wonder if you've ever heard of Augustus John? He is a reality, though a terrific one. His drawings are triumphant – both in execution and filth. He's an abominable man, lives as if he were a gipsy, had two wives until the other day he took a third, on which the first two quarreled with him, and one of them died as she was producing a child – and is in fact a typical artist. Henry Lamb and his prostitute wife have clung onto his menage, and a few weeks ago they all went over to Paris, where they were seen to be rolling down the boulevards drunk, in a long line down the street. The complications of their copulations became intense, and at last they all quarreled, all threatened to kill each other and commit suicide, and eventually all went off in different directions. "Nina" as she is called (Henry's lady) was left behind without a penny, and

Augustus John, *The Supplicant*, *c.* 1907, graphite on paper

with nothing to do but prey upon Duncan. This she certainly did, though to what extent, and in what way, still remains a mystery. I shouldn't be at all surprised to hear that he was keeping her – oh! In every meaning of the word. But what does it matter?'

Lytton would certainly been jealous of Duncan and Euphemia's relationship, as he himself was in love with Duncan. Although they were cousins, they had entered a sexual relationship a few months previously. Duncan was bisexual and promiscuous.

The affair with Duncan was over by June. Euphemia remained friends with many of her lovers for the rest of her life. Not so Duncan. One must assume that on this occasion Euphemia was the promiscuous one and dallied abroad. Duncan wrote cattily to Lytton's brother James about Euphemia:

> 'Henry has left Nina perhaps for ever and the white haired whore still goes on eating "crème nouvettes".'

Crème nouvettes is a French dish of carrots in cream and 'eating crème nouvettes' was a colloquial expression for fellatio.

There was a sexual liaison between Euphemia and Augustus John, but the exact timing is not known. Following the Henry Lamb and Dorelia affair, John was pragmatic:

> 'Could we not form a discreet colony… in couples… For the sake of symmetry, I could double as myself no doubt at suitable intervals.'

The relationship with Augustus John was one of the most important of Euphemia's life, both artistically and in terms of friendship and support. They maintained a close relationship until her death. In the aftermath of the Henry/Dorelia elopement, Euphemia continued to model for Augustus John and, interestingly, during this period the drawings John did of her take on a new quality. The insatiable John continued to be inspired by Euphemia and renamed her 'Lobelia'. Unlike Lamb, John was able to capture Euphemia's sexuality in a pure way. The heads both artists drew of her in London are angelic. In Paris, John began to respond to Euphemia and her body, both clothed and nude, in a new way, capturing her unashamed eroticism. In his biography of John, Michael Holroyd argues that John relied on 'some

William Rothenstein, *Augustus John*, 1899, oil on canvas, 77 x 56.2 cm

extreme instinctive relationship' between himself and his subject and that when he painted women, this was 'almost impossible to achieve if his concentration was constantly fretted by unsatisfied physical desire'. Whatever the means, John managed to capture what Baudelaire said it was the artist's job to convey: the 'come-hitherishness' of the unchaste woman. Euphemia's unique talent as an artist's model was to be able to withstand the scrutiny of the male gaze and always be her natural and unselfconscious self.

One of the attractions of Euphemia as a model was that she was very fair, with pale skin and blonde hair. Augustus John wrote to Henry Lamb:

'I don't seem to come across fair women.'[1]

John wrote to his mistress Alick Schepeler back in London:

'I have simply taken her for granted. It is true I have thought her rather eccentric.'

Her body was a revelation; he was exploring its muscularity and monumentality, her asexual and androgynous allure.
John also wrote to Lamb:

'She [Lobelia] makes an irresistible boy.'[2]

He drew her repeatedly and, in this way, she achieved some financial independence. Writing about an old portrait of Schepeler that he had found, John commented to Lamb that what he found remarkable about it was that:

'Her face embodies all that is corrupt – but then has a monumental character and the pose is perfect.'[3]

Dorelia returned to John and the children, whilst Henry went on a walking tour for several months. Henry Lamb and Augustus John remained friends, and John even requested Lamb to come and visit to improve Dorelia's spirit:

'I look forward to your coming here – Dorelia, will I hope buck up under your sunny influence. Yours is evidently the touch. I trust the gallant Lobelia (no offence) will be no obstacle to your coming.'[4]

---

1. Augustus John, letter to Henry Lamb, Tate Archives, TAM 15B 39/52.
2. Augustus John, letter to Henry Lamb, 6 July 1907, Tate Archives, TAM 15B 39/52.
3. Augustus John, letter to Henry Lamb, September 1907, Tate Archives, TAM 6/7/07.
4. Augustus John, letter to Henry Lamb, August 1907, Tate Archives, TAM 15B 35/52.

In their frequent correspondence to each other, John reported on Euphemia's whereabouts to Lamb or requested information about her. In July 1907 he wrote to Lamb:

> 'Your spouse is here with the Swede lying ill in a mechant hotel... Having fled with Hugo [the Swede], in the guise of a youth intending to proceed to the Maeterlincks – she had the impulse to break the journey by spending a few hours in Bretagne... Lobelia says she does not want you to come, her high temperature would probably rise still higher – on the other hand she is sending for a German who it appears exercises a soothing influence on her. Her Swede finds it imperative to return to Paris today.'

Café society was an important aspect of bohemian Paris. The cafés, in addition to providing food and drink, also provided tables at which people could think and write, and a social circle. The collegiate environment allowed socialisation and the pursuance of professional interests. Poets and writers could find like-minded intellectuals to discuss ideas, and artist's models like Euphemia could find work. We know that in addition to Augustus John and Duncan Grant, she was modelling for Rudolph Grossman, Charles Winzer, Maresco Pearce and Jules Adler. Another character who was in Paris at this time was the cartoonist Max Beerbohm. Max was sitting next to John in the Au Café de la Tartine Parisienne while Augustus John was writing a letter to Dorelia about Lobelia's antics at the Bal des Quat'z'Arts. Max sketched a caricature of some of the dozens of awful art students in the background onto John's letter. Beerbohm is best known for his novel *Zuleika Dobson*, the story of a girl arriving in Oxford and promptly causing every male in the town to fall in love with her through her magnetism. Did some of Euphemia's magnetism find its way into the characterisation of Zuleika Dobson? Certainly, Euphemia was becoming a bit of a 'celebrity' in the Paris demi-monde.

Henry returned from Italy in June 1907 and Euphemia continued to help him out financially until he was back on his feet.

Augustus John, *Girl dressing her hair*, *c.* 1907, graphite on paper, 54.8 x 35.7 cm

Duncan wrote to Lytton in June 1907:

'Henry Lamb is back from his walk and has been working at
La Palette so that I have seen a good deal of him. He is very
interesting and plays on the piano very well indeed. His wife
in his absence has been living with a charming Swedish youth,
whom I nearly fell in love with. He's very stupid, but well off and
wants to marry her, but as she's Henry's only support I believe
he's against it. But of how much he is ignorant is a mystery.'

Following Henry's infidelity with Dorelia, Euphemia first took
Duncan as a lover and then moved on to the handsome Swede.

The Swede seems to have been a literary man; he was en route with
Euphemia to visit the Maeterlincks (the Belgian playwright Maurice
Maeterlinck and his mistress Georgette LeBlanc) when Euphemia fell
ill. Also, Augustus John wrote to Henry Lamb that the Swede was a
friend of William Butler Yeats, the Irish poet:

'I wonder what has become of Lobelia. Yeats the poet was
talking to me about a man he knew in Paris who I realised was
none other than the Swede.'[5]

Duncan Grant, who was in Florence in the summer of 1908, wrote
to Lytton Strachey:

'I had tea with Vanessa and Clive today and they told me that
Henry Lamb and Nina were coming back to England. I wonder
if he is tearing her away from the beautiful Swede. It has often
occurred to me that he (the Swede) must be very interesting,
but whenever I've talked to him, I've been unable to believe
that anything he said was sincere… I used always to fall back
on his beauty, and that of course is interesting enough. But I
wish I knew more about his mind.'

5. Augustus John, letter to Henry Lamb, August 1907, Tate Archives, TAM 15B 35/52.

The Swede wanted to marry her but Euphemia was not interested in marriage, nor was she available to marry. The affair continued on and off for several months, with Lamb and John believing she was destined to go to Finland with him. Ultimately, he could not tolerate the other men and she wrote that the 'Swede', who was extremely jealous and angry, had walked away.

In this period following Lamb's desertion of her, Euphemia was learning the rewards of sex. That sex was power, that it had the ability to make men interested in her and keep them attentive and loving. The romance of enrapturing men attracted her.

Henry Lamb wrote to Augustus John asking after Euphemia in July 1907. John responded:

'I know nothing of Euphemia's doings I regret. I trust she has not taken herself out of sight.'[6]

A month later in August 1907, John had some news:

'She [Euphemia] has made the acquaintance of a number of nations!'

From now on Euphemia was in her element – everyone was keen to make her acquaintance, and she used her influence to educate herself and have some excellent adventures.

---

6. Henry Lamb, letter to Augustus John, Tate Archives, 15TAM.

Augustus John, *Euphemia Lamb*, pencil on paper, 35 x 23 cm

SIX

A Threesome

Her skin, her shape, her kind of childish madness,
sometimes stupid, sometimes brilliant, pleased me,
but not the men around her or her cavalier manner with them.
– Henri-Pierre Roché

IN THE SUMMER OF 1907, in her long velvet cape, Euphemia sat down next to the French writer Henri-Pierre Roché at the Café du Dome. He was reading a book and ignored her. When his friend Franz Hessel arrived, he laughed at the incongruity of the situation and they became acquainted. Roché had decided to make his life's work the study of the relationship between men and women, from an intellectual, social, sexual and moral perspective. He and Hessel were great friends, they were attracted to the same sort of women but wanted different things from their experiences. In the previous year (1906) Roché had introduced his mistress, the painter Marie Laurencin, to Hessel and they thenceforth shared a sexual relationship with her until she left them both for the writer and poet Apollinaire. The idea of a triangular relationship interested the men and Euphemia entered into this arrangement.

Roché wrote in his diary:

> 'At the café, little Ofe [Roché's pet name for Euphemia] speaks to me. I have seen her for two months here and there, without almost knowing her, with her husband – a painter, who does not seem to care about her, with a young Scandinavian, sweet and strong, whom she seems to love like a lover, and with Adler [Jules Adler – artist]. Their bohemianism reaches the extreme limit. Ofe is 18 years old, snowy flesh, periwinkle eyes, long blonde hair, a rich, fresh, pink mouth. She wraps herself in a vast cape of black cloth, her bare feet in monks'

sandals. Her skin, her shape, her kind of childish madness, sometimes stupid, sometimes brilliant, pleased me, but not the men around her or her cavalier manner with them... Today we were alone, she stood next to me, behaved so I could read. Then she spoke indiscriminately of her husband, of her lover, of Adler. I remained suspicious. Glob [Hessel] arrived immediately and laughed with Ofe. We invited her to have tea at his place. She said yes.'[1]

Augustus John, *Portrait of Euphemia Lamb*, pencil and wash, 48.9 x 29.2 cm

At Hessel's flat they gave her a French lesson:

'All three of us sitting on Glob's bed, we give Ofe a French lesson, and she applies it, funny enough. We are respectful. Sometimes Glob kisses her arm. I lay down in the alley with her head resting on my side... At this moment I am only thinking of Ofe. I pull her head higher, close to mine and I continue the lesson by speaking into her little ear and then kissing it. Ofe smells of the fragrance of apples. We plan another lesson for tomorrow.'[2]

The lesson was repeated the next day, but Hessel left early so that Roché and Euphemia could become better acquainted. Roché wrote:

---

1. Henri-Pierre Roché, diary, 21 July 1907, Harry Ransom Center, University of Texas, Carnet 38.
2. Ibid

'Second French lesson with Ofe, on Glob's bed. Little by little Glob withdrew and began to write, with his back turned. Ofe is pushed against me, more serious. I am surprised by her and exhilarated. Her arm goes around my neck… Our mouths meet. Her arched Apollonian mouth, like a Rosetti has a volume of lips.'[3]

Roché was entranced:

'The naivety and simplicity of repetition of Ofe's lips touch me. Our beautiful emotion rose straight up. She is suddenly the completely white, white haired, elongated, full figured woman I never had. Ofe undid my collar, had her cheek on my bare chest. She slips under the blanket, lets go of her bodice and skirt. Her periwinkle eyes are serious and wanting.

"Won't Glob get angry?" she asks.

The back of Glob over there would turn around for nothing in the world. I go to him.

"Should I go out?" he asks kindly in a low voice.

Glob is gone. Dear Glob. We are alone. Naked. She is supple, fragrant, fresh apple. She is eighteen years old. Her beauty runs from her feet to her hands. Her breasts are a little tilted, because of a dead baby. She simply offers herself. I can't take her. Waiting for her hurts. I have to familiarise myself. I would like to take time to learn her. I can't because I find her pretty, fine, delicate and malleable. You would have to be very sure of yourself to push straight into the centre of beauty… We know each other a little and we laugh.'[4]

Henri-Pierre Roché was a connoisseur of sex and seduction. He kept a diary of all his sexual activities for over sixty years and there were many conquests. However, his ability to describe in great detail his amorous activities is invaluable in helping us get a sense of Euphemia as a lover

---

3. Henri-Pierre Roché, diary, 22 July 1907, Harry Ransom Center, University of Texas.
4. Ibid.

Photograph of Henri-Pierre Roché, 1930s

and as a friend and as a person. Their sexual entanglement lasted for about a year, but they continued to write to each other for twenty-five years. She preferred him to her other lovers, but I think she realised that he was never going to be completely available, and she certainly made no efforts (despite her protestations) to stay faithful to him. As with Henry Lamb, she was interested in his mind and what he could teach her. He introduced her to the writings of Shakespeare, Sterne, Swinburne and Rabelais. Further French lessons led to an improvement in her ability to communicate:

> 'Her French vocabulary improves, but luckily not her grammar.
> She does not like me to speak English to her.'

Roché found her ungrammatical pidgin French amusing and her 'infantile type of craziness, sometimes stupid, sometimes brilliant, pleased me'. He later immortalised her and her way of expressing herself and her antics in his account of Odile in several chapters of his famous novel *Jules et Jim* (1953):

'She was called Odile and she liked coming to drink tea with them in Jules' flat; he lived near the café. She said she had married and divorced; she spoke pidgin; she was direct, brutally frank, full of humour and had skin like milk.

"Me no understand life men women here. Be opposite to my country. Them here make love when want. This important. Me want learn here."'

In the novel, Jules (Hessel) helps Odile (Euphemia) seduce Jim (Roché):

'They took their dominoes. Jim arrived and they drank tea. Odile set about her seduction scene like a clown, putting on an

Franz Hessel, photograph of Franz Hessel and Euphemia kissing, Holland, August 1907

act for Jules and for herself too. Jim lent himself to it without knowing what it was all about. Odile had liked him at first sight… she quickly had him in fits of laughter, holding his sides and gasping.'

At a pre-arranged time, Odile gave Jules a signal to leave his own flat and the seduction of Jim took place:

'The next day Jules et Jim, both working in Jules' flat, heard a high spirited Yoop! Yoop! through the open window. It was Odile passing by accompanied by a tall young man who was a compatriot of hers. She had monks' sandals on her bare feet, a long black Spanish cloak, and a big dark blue straw hat of the kind worn by the Salvation Army.'

Odile is described as coming to the flat regularly and she was always welcome; ostensibly it was to improve her French with a native speaker. There is a description of her taking Jim to her place, a three-roomed apartment opening on to a cul-de-sac in an old house in a humble quarter. Two rooms are described as empty but the third contained a mattress on the floor and some embroidered blankets and pillows. Next to the bed was a row of furry creatures, old and new, which she would freely talk to and play with when in his company. It transpired that she had been selling off her things slowly after her husband had left her.

Roché and Hessel called Euphemia 'Ofe', a reference to Ophelia. The siren quality to her nature where she exploited her beauty and her sexuality was captured by Roché in his short story, *Don Juan et la Petite Sirène* (1909). The *petite sirène* is a mermaid who lures the protagonist to ecstasy and physical union in a playful and flirtatious manner (see Appendix A).

Henri-Pierre Roché and Franz Hessel both subscribed to Baudelaire's manifesto for the flâneur. They were men about town and knew everyone. Roché had met Gertrude Stein, the American art collector and writer, at Kathleen Bruce's studio in Paris. In *The Autobiography of Alice B. Toklas*, Stein describes him thus:

Photograph of Gertrude Stein sitting on a sofa in her Paris studio, 1930

'Roché was one of those characters that are always to be found in Paris. He was a very earnest, very noble, devoted, very faithful and very enthusiastic man who was a general introducer. He knew everybody, he really knew them and he could introduce anybody to anybody. He lived with his mother and grandmother. Later he was often at 27 rue de Fleuris with various nationalities and Gertrude Stein rather liked him. She always said of him he is so faithful. Gertrude mentioned at Kathleen Bruce's studio that she had just bought a picture by Picasso. Good, good, excellent, said Roché, he is a very interesting young fellow, I know him. Oh do you, said Gertrude Stein, well enough to take somebody to see him? Why certainly said Roché. Shortly after Roché and Gertrude Stein and her brother went to see Picasso.'

There were plenty of Englishmen at Gertrude's soirées, including Augustus John and Henry Lamb. She described John as 'not too sober' and Lamb as 'rather strange and attractive.'

Roché took Euphemia to weekly literary meetings at the Closerie des Lilas, where writers such as Paul Fort and André Salmon were in attendance. He encouraged Euphemia to read widely and their letters talk about books they had bought for each other.

Like Odile in *Jules et Jim*, Euphemia's relations with Roché and Hessel were tempestuous. Roché recalled her waking up from a sleep in Hessel's apartment:

'She says my name, opens her eyes, pulls me close and snuggles. Her awakening ends under my kisses. Her cheerfulness bursts. She jumps up, beats me, beats Glob [Hessel], half loses her shirt, tears it off completely and hits us with it, so hard that I have to hold her back. I carry her in my arms, she struggles, bites me, kisses me.'[5]

One morning in July, Roché found her sitting on the bottom of his stairs, on the concierge's folding chair, with her diabolo on her knees. Euphemia told him that she had been woken up at 5am that morning by the Swede to whom she had written she was ill, and had fallen asleep on her chair. At 6am another friend arrived, a painter who asked her to

5. Henri-Pierre Roché, diary, 24 July 1907, Harry Ransom Center, University of Texas.

Franz Hessel, photograph of Euphemia reading outside, Holland, August 1907

model. But instead she chose to go to the Luxembourg Gardens where she threw her diabolo higher than all the others. This gives us a sense of her child-like capricious and impulsive nature and how she was adept at keeping several lovers on the go at the same time.

Roché describes the actual moment of love-making:

> 'She gives herself with cheerfulness and tenderness. She is terribly restless and muscular. She reaps ecstasies and brings others back to life.'

During their love affair, Roché was also seeing his other lover Germaine Bonnard, who he called Vieve in his diary. She would remain his long-term partner throughout his many other affairs.

Euphemia was also sleeping with her errant husband during this time. This is humorously captured in *Jules et Jim* when Odile announces that she would like him to meet her ex-husband:

> 'She took him to a long, narrow, glazed studio. The ex-husband was very young, on the effeminate side, and spoke quickly and precisely; Jim rather liked him. They drank tea, played chess and drew their game; Odile, who was totally ignorant of chess, gave them both advice. The ex-husband said to Jim:
>
> "Odile has told me about you and I know what place you occupy in her life. Congratulations. Only I ought to let you know that during the last few days, as it happens, Odile and I have revived the past and resumed marital relations."
>
> Jim had a glimpse of a stool flying backwards and Odile flying forwards almost horizontally, stretched out like a spring released, with her merciless little hands reaching out to seize her ex-husband by the throat and hurl him over backwards.'

In order to appease Jim after this revelation, Roché writes a seduction scene which elucidates Euphemia's *modus operandi* when she was caught being unfaithful:

> 'It was cold. "We'll make a big fire," she said. She undressed, sat down naked on the floor with her legs apart and a foot pressed against the wall on each side of the fireplace, grabbed lumps of coal from the scuttles, knocked them happily against one another, talking to them meanwhile and covering the carpet with black splinters, and in less than no time had built a high, roaring fire. As she had rubbed her hands on her body now and then, she was striped with black. She asked Jim to put the light out, and in the glow from the fire amused herself.'

In this way she set about making Jim forget the scene with her ex-husband.

Franz Hessel, photograph of Euphemia on the dunes, Holland, August 1907

Roché and Hessel proposed a trip to Holland with Euphemia in August 1907. They were unsure whether she would actually come. The arrangement between Roché and Hessel was that they often shared their girlfriends. The nature of their threesome is explored in the chapter 'Among the Dunes' in *Jules et Jim*, where Jim returns to the hotel and finds Odile and Jules asleep in their respective beds:

'The light woke her. "Me good girl, me go to bed by myself" she said. Jules came in shaking a finger at her: "Because me no want you in my bed," "You being stupid" said Odile "You not understand me want be in your bed because me not have animals and me not like sleep all alone… but me good girl for Jim!" "But maybe me not good boy!" put in Jules. She stared at him outraged.'

Franz Hessel, photograph of naked Euphemia cooking, Holland, August 1907

During this trip, Euphemia asked Roché's permission to go and sleep with Hessel. However, Roché recorded in his diary that although Hessel and Euphemia were great friends, there wasn't much sexual attraction between them. Hessel joked with Euphemia that he only liked men, but in fact he visited the nearby town to frequent the brothel on a couple of occasions. Euphemia's antics meant that she was often a handful and it was good for the two men to have each other to control her:

'Sometimes she's mean and selfish, wants to buy everything in town. Sometimes she's brutal and savage and treacherous. You have to get a little angry. Glob has some authority over her when I don't.'[6]

6. Henri-Pierre Roché, diary, 20 September 1907, Harry Ransom Center, University of Texas.

The three of them found a small, isolated house in the dunes not far from the sea. Downstairs there was a large room with a mattress for Roché and Euphemia to sleep on and next to it a room that became a kitchen and a toilet. Hessel occupied the attic above. They stayed there for three weeks. Euphemia looked after the house:

> 'To our surprise, Ofe kept her word and was a first-rate housekeeper and cook… When dinner was ready she would shout "My birds!" and we would come down from the attic. She would stuff us with good things and watch us eat, keeping only the least beautiful things for herself. At the end of the meal, Glob became "Gustave" and made the coffee, I became "Jean" and served, she became "Suzanne" and washed the dishes.'

They bathed naked on a remote bit of the beach away from the cabins.

SEVEN

Café Cocotte

Her bohemianism reaches the extreme limit.
Throwing away her little money, the refined
and dangerous wretch. – Henri-Pierre Roché

THIS PERIOD FOLLOWING THE TRIP to Holland is one of the only times we get to hear a first-hand account of Euphemia's life, as she penned seventy letters to Henri-Pierre Roché. Some are accounts of what she was up to whilst he was travelling in Germany and abroad; others are notes written when they were both in Paris and she continued to write once she had returned to London. They offer us an insight into the messy and chaotic side of her life.

After the trip to Holland, Hessel and Roché continued on to Germany and Euphemia reluctantly returned to Paris. She had let go of her room, so Roché offered to put her up in a hotel. She went to the Hotel Delambre and struck up a relationship with the German artist Rudolph Grossman. She became his model and girlfriend and when she ran out of money, she moved in with him to his apartment at 6 rue Vercingetorix. They were very poor. In the middle of September, Euphemia was writing to Roché in Germany:

> 'Me went to Grossman studio, me no money to pay hotel. Me pose for sculptor mais il etait tres mechant aveck moi if I don't pose again. Grossman and I no sleep, separate beds, no money to eat.'[1]

She even drew a diagram of the bedroom, indicating the separate beds; however, the week before she had explicitly informed Roché that

---

1. Euphemia Lamb, letter to Henri–Pierre Roché, 15 Sept. 1907, Harry Ransom Center, Univ. of Texas.

'kiss moi beaucoup because apres il [Grossman] demande moi sleep apres moi no know.'[2]

Roché was phlegmatic about this affair:

'She became the mistress of Roos [Grossman]. In her first letters she claimed not to sleep with him. She even gave me a plan of the studio showing the distance between the beds. I quite like this choice. Roos has a strong face that one might find beautiful. No blandness. His body, which I have seen often, is very white, muscular with reddish gold hair. He is silent, not rich. The idea that he takes her hardly damages her for me.'

Euphemia wrote to Roché:

'We don't eat every day but we play very well and I'm starting to really love him.'

Roché evidently sent her some money to pay for the hotel and food, as a week later she wrote:

'Moi mange beaucoup maintenant.'[3]

Roché was attracted to the wild and uninhibited aspect of Euphemia's personality, but it entailed a high degree of chaos, and his regular trips abroad and stays in a sanatorium might indicate that he found her exhausting. When Roché returned to Paris, he was anxious about seeing the couple and wrote in his diary:

'There they are on the terrace of a café. Roos smiling, friendly, Ofe sitting near me but with a large man's fedora so pressed on her head and her face so lowered that I don't see her eyes or mouth.

2. Euphemia Lamb, letter to Henri-Pierre Roché, 6 Sept. 1907, Harry Ransom Center, Univ. of Texas.
3. Euphemia Lamb, letter to Henri-Pierre Roché, 25 Sept. 1907, Harry Ransom Center, Univ. of Texas.

Franz Hessel, photograph of Euphemia and Roché embracing, Holland, August 1907

"Do you love her?" Roos asked me with irony.
"But yes," replied Roché.'

Euphemia suggested to Roché that they sleep together to check whether they still loved each other. She was careful not to cause a rift between the two men, and continued to sleep with them both.

'Each of us is very fond of her, but each hesitates to take responsibility for all her little mad moments.'[4]

---

4. Henri-Pierre Roché, diary, Harry Ransom Center, University of Texas.

Roché found the two of them:

'... a nice old room, all tiled, which she liked, with furniture so
broken that the owner had nothing to fear from Ofe. The bed
was huge with thick sheets. The window overlooked a courtyard
with climbing vines. It was there that little by little I managed
to sleep every night – and our love regained all its strength.
In the early days she sometimes had expeditions with Roos
who now lived in Montmartre. Then our tenderness increased
and she declared that she loved me and wanted to be faithful
to me and showed me as proof, complaining letters from Roos.'

When Euphemia was in Paris entertaining several lovers on an
evening out, she would make it clear which lover she intended to go
home with by giving the appointed one her bottle of milk to carry home.
When Roché travelled again, Euphemia returned to Grossman.

Franz Hessel, photograph of Euphemia washing, Holland, August 1907

Paul Gauguin, *Portrait of William Molard*, 1894, oil on canvas, 46 x 38 cm

Grossman lived upstairs from a musician named William Molard and a Swedish sculptress named Ida Ericsson. They had been living there for several years and a previous occupant of Grossman's apartment had been Paul Gauguin. Gauguin had painted two portraits of Molard. Euphemia and Grossman became friends with them and at the beginning of December 1907 Euphemia wrote that:

'... me unhappy, Swedish woman and her husband are very kind to me. We were very drunk last night. Me sleep alone. I am petite virgin.'[5]

---

5. Euphemia Lamb, letter to Henri-Pierre Roché, 2 December 1907, Harry Ransom Center, Univ. of Texas.

A few days later Euphemia had become embroiled with the couple:

'... poor petit homme moi trusts pour lui moi... dans ma bouche mois kiss doucement, petit femme fache avec moi, elle pense ma fault, elle no avec son mari, mais elle no knows.'

Euphemia and Molard had kissed and Ida was displeased and blamed Euphemia. Euphemia sought consolation with Grossman.

'Moi hate Rudie... Rudie is in Montmartre now – he demand sleep avec moi pour une semaine parce que son lit est mauvais.'[6]

In this period before Christmas 1907 Euphemia appeared to be living fast and loose. Grossman seems to have become involved with another cocotte called Monasse and in an attempt to make him jealous, Euphemia had seduced his downstairs neighbour. She wrote regularly at this time to Roché while he was in Berlin staying with Hessel, at his mother's house. She wrote Roché a brutal letter about her situation:

'You are quite wrong if you think I don't write because I'm not a virgin still. I wouldn't sleep with anyone here as I hate everyone. I hate you and pudding [Hessel]. You are all selfish. The men here say why should I give her money, she always slept with Roché when he was here. You only think whether she's fidèle or not it doesn't matter if I have my dejeuner or dinner or pay my rent. It's just vulgar to discuss money so I will stop.'[7]

Euphemia's lifestyle was tremendous fun with lots of lovers and attention, but also sordid and destructive. She was a twenty-year-old woman trying to survive in a foreign city without any security other than that offered to her by her work as a model and by men such as Roché who offered to support her.

---

6. Euphemia Lamb, letter to Henri-Pierre Roché, 10 December 1907, Harry Ransom Center, Univ. of Texas.
7. Euphemia Lamb, letter to Henri-Pierre Roché, 20 December 1907, Harry Ransom Center, Univ. of Texas.

Euphemia sent her own letter describing the fun that she had had at the Café Versailles on Christmas Eve:

'I danced in Café Versailles and I had on a beautiful silver grey dress, it is one my mother gave me, it is very decollete and fell off my shoulders. Everyone said I was beautiful or pretty. Madame Paul Fort was very gracious and said some nice things, Paul Fort was very silly and said he loved me and swore he would kill you. Marias was silly too. I danced with the tall dark woman who is nearly always at Versailles. She is beautiful. Of course half of Paris is talking about me now but it wasn't the night at Versailles that did it. Do come back soon. I stay here until the 8th January.'[8]

The fact that Roché was away during this period exacerbated her instability; she does seem to have been bereft at his absence and in all her letters she was pleading for him to return. Also, she was still reeling from Henry Lamb's desertion of her only five months previously. In fact, at this period of crisis it was Henry Lamb who came to the rescue. He visited her on Christmas Day 1907 and found her ill in bed and miserable. He decided to write to Roché to see what could be done. His letter summarises her predicament well:

'Dear Roché,
I am sorry to tell you that Euphemia is ill again. Of course this is nothing but the natural result of the rash life she leads. I found her in bed yesterday evening in a miserable state, ill with no one to care for her and feeling generally desolate.
After a lengthy discussion I succeeded in making her promise not to continue her career as a café "star"; but this is just where the difficulty begins. She doesn't want to go to Finland on the 8th January (as she had proposed) but appears willing enough for some sort of change. She asked me to write

---

8. Euphemia Lamb, letter to Henri-Pierre Roché, 28 December 1907, Harry Ransom Center, Univ. of Texas.

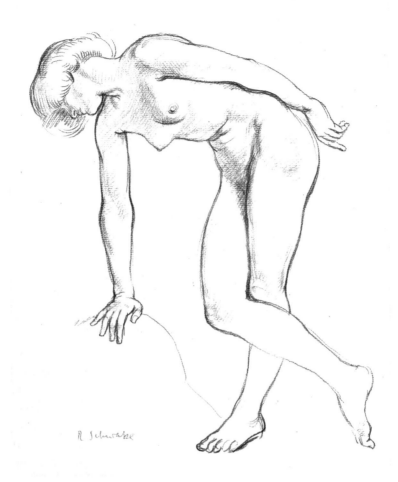

Randolphe Schwabe, *Euphemia nude*, c. 1905, charcoal on paper

to you informing you of her illness, fearing that you would not credit her own story; at the same time I can assure you that you are not to attach too much importance to the various injurious letters she has sent you; and that she really is very anxious to see you again.

Accordingly I am to ask you if you can suggest anything: you see she is utterly bored with her life here and doesn't know what to do with herself. As far as I can make out, I think she would like very much to be with you in Germany.

One suggestion of hers was that we should all three of us go to our cottage in England: but personally I can't think that this would be a very successful trio! Moreover I am particularly anxious not to leave my work here just now.

I am feeling very perplexed and fear that I have underrated my responsibility. She says now that she detests everyone. "Elle ne possible que vous et moi."

Well in the meantime I am pinning my hope on some practical suggestion from you.

The indisposition is nothing serious, but her general state of health appears extremely feeble.

With kindest regards to yourself and remembrance to Hessel,

I am yours very sincerely,

Henry Lamb

She sends you her love.'[9]

At around this time an American couple who were both artists employed Euphemia as a model. Rather like the situation in Jean Rhys' novel *Quartet*, they took on a parental role with Euphemia where they not only painted her but became emotionally involved and lavished money on her and tried to rescue her from her bohemian ways. Roché, in his diary, referred to them as the Puritans. Euphemia claimed that the husband was in love with her and she showed Roché the frequent letters from the woman which exhibited a mystical tenderness and exalted love and friendship towards her. When she was regularly late to their studio, they gave her a watch. According to Roché they 'painted her everyday at their house, they bought her bourgeois dresses and everything she wanted. They wanted her conversion. At first this went well.' But she treated them badly. There were quarrels, tears from the woman and anger from the man and rage and resentment from Euphemia. The long sittings at their house had occupied her days and when the relationship ended, she was at another loose end.

---

9. Henry Lamb, letter to Henri–Pierre Roché, 28 December 1907, Harry Ransom Center, Univ. of Texas.

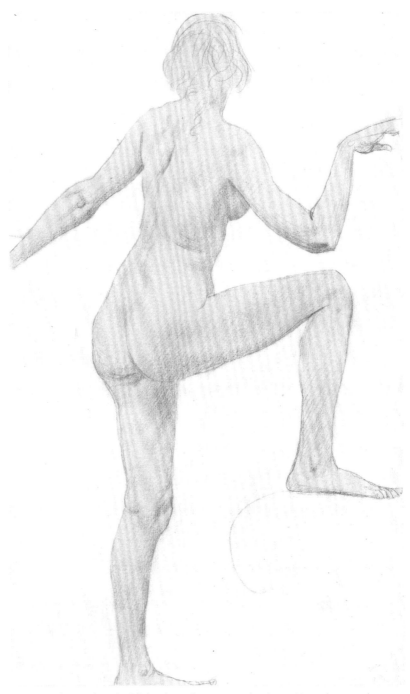

Augustus John, *Nude study: full-length, one foot resting on bench*, graphite and grey wash on paper, 40.5 x 25.3 cm

Also at this time, Euphemia met a tall, handsome, strong young English aristocrat who made an apartment available to Euphemia. At first Euphemia thought she was going to like him a lot; they were together all the time. He took her out and showed her to all his friends. According to Roché, the English lord made love to her incessantly; however, Euphemia found him too sporty and did not enjoy the sex as much as she had with Roché.

Euphemia told Roché, 'I had so much fun. I was very rich – always in a car and dresses. I know all the very expensive restaurants that you don't know.' She also thought him crazy and narrowly avoided injury in a car accident. He wanted her to have sex with another woman whilst he watched and then they began to quarrel. After her big night at the Bal des Quat'z'Arts in 1908 where she spent the night with the Russian (known as Prince George), she also then went to bed with the English lord later that day.

One of the outcomes of Henry Lamb's letter to Roché asking for some practical suggestion that could help put Euphemia on an even keel was an introduction to his Russian friend Nikolai Semenov. Born in 1883, Semenov had once been the ballet master of the Imperial Moscow Theatre in Russia. He had come to Paris to join Diaghilev's Ballets Russes, where he was the administrator for the choreographer Michel Fokine. Roché thought that Euphemia could help him learn French and English. Semenov became a regular fixture in her life over the next six months and she did become more financially secure. However, her promise to leave the life of a café star behind her was not achieved.

Semenov was married with three daughters; his family lived at Badenweiler in the Black Forest in Germany. Roché would go and stay with Semenov and his family there. Semenov was robust and able to tolerate some of Euphemia's extremes. When she became extremely drunk and started vomiting, Semenov took control. He knew exactly how to take care of drunks; wet towels, shower on the back of the neck, pressure on the stomach and helped to disgorge. He commented, 'Excellent, I like women like that. She drank to the end, she goes to the end. Afterwards she will be hungry. She doesn't make a fuss. I don't like women who pretend to be drunk.' After this episode Euphemia and Semenov started to spend evenings together. He told his good friend Roché that 'Now we are brothers-in-law!' which in Russian meant that he had slept with her. Semenov also showered her with gifts and bought her anything she wanted. Euphemia was getting a taste for the high life. Semenov and Roché invited Euphemia to come on a walking tour to the Black Forest in August 1908; she never went because she had decided to return to London. In later life Semenov lost his entire family in the 1917 Revolution, emigrated to the United States and ran a dance school in Cleveland, Ohio. After his livelihood was threatened by the Depression of the 1930s, he committed suicide by throwing himself over Niagara Falls in Canada.

Euphemia boasted to Roché that 'she only slept with his friends'. Roché tolerated her infidelities and was of course not faithful himself. He prided himself on being an experienced and expert lover and their love-making seems to have been inspired by various jealousies and rivalries that infidelity created. Roché commented:

> 'I only feel melancholy for a moment; she does it with so much grace – like a mistress of the house who does the honours of her garden. And when I am there, afterwards she gives me such preference in front of them, they become jealous.'

Euphemia was very pragmatic about her other lovers:

> 'I imagine that you [Roché] must have slept with 40-50 women in your life. When I have slept with that many men, we will be even. I will have experience and I will begin to be faithful.'[10]

She had learned tit for tat from her marriage with Henry Lamb:

> 'Give me a good example. You know that making love with a lot of people isn't what makes you happy. I'm not always

10. Henri–Pierre Roché, diary, Harry Ransom Center, University of Texas, Carnet 44.

faithful because I'm very young and a louse but help me become faithful.'[11]

Roché commented that their lovemaking was:

'... based on the experience of our bodies and her experience is far more restricted than mine. I know including her husband, Grossman, Hessel, Semenov and the Lord about ten men that she slept with. I suspect 4 or 5 more. I know most of these men. I have never felt my Little Man [his penis] threatened.'[12]

Euphemia played men at their own game and often won. Her freedom was that she appeared not to become too emotionally involved with them. She seems to have loved Henry Lamb and Henri-Pierre Roché, but maybe that was because they tolerated and enjoyed the experience of sharing her with others. Her sexual availability and unsentimental attitude to her lovers may have been born out of emotional neglect and a feeling of being unloved in childhood. As soon as she became aware of her allure and the power she had over men, Euphemia may have compensated by becoming promiscuous in her attachments. She was afraid of becoming pregnant but there were many pregnancies and many terminations. One of her doctors recommended that when she was pregnant, the biggest chance of miscarriage would occur by 'frothing', i.e. having sex with as many men as possible. As Roché laconically wrote in his diary, 'it was her fate to never know exactly who made her pregnant'. In one of her letters to him after he had sent her money for a *femme sage* to procure an illegal operation, he wrote that he felt she might be trying to extort money from him; she replied that whilst she did that with the other lovers, she wouldn't do that to him, because she loved him. Even though he may have been her preferred lover, Roché was not a rich man and her experiences in Paris made her realise that she enjoyed luxury and finery.

11. Ibid.
12. Ibid.

Walter Lamb wrote to Clive Bell in April 1908, summarising Euphemia's situation:

'I found my brother, who appears to be doing some very fine drawings but to be making no money and to be under the necessity of changing his abode about twice a week; whereas his wife, while changing her friends about every ten days, persuades them to maintain her always in the same set of rooms. She seems to be on fairly amicable terms with him but is meditating divorce.'[13]

Bal des Quat'z'Arts 1908

The annual Bal des Quat'z'Arts was a costume ball which was given every year in the spring by the students of the different ateliers of painting, architecture and sculpture. Tickets were difficult to come by and even if secured did not ensure admittance. One had to pass a masked jury to ensure that one's costume was of sufficient artistic originality to gain entrance. There would be floats of moving tableaux depicting various scenes: the Stone Age and primitive man, or the last days of Babylon amongst others. Admission was between 10pm and midnight and the ball lasted all night. The committee of the ball awarded prizes to females who distinguished themselves by the artistic merit and beauty of their female display. All the women who competed for these prizes were to be lined up on the grand staircase before the orchestra. Roché described how 'an expert woman took Euphemia home for an hour and brought me back an Egyptian Princess with large veils. She later took off the blue veils and was the naked lunar queen.'

In *Jules et Jim*, Roché looks back at this period in 1908 when he and Hessel enjoyed the café society of Paris; he includes a description of the 1908 Bal des Quat'z'Arts:

'Jim and Jules took Lucie and Odile to the Bal des Quat-z-Arts.

---

13. Walter Lamb, letter to Clive Bell, April 1908, Tate Archives.

Invitation card for women to the Bal des Quat'z'Arts, 1908

Lucie was dressed as a priestess; For the first hour Odile
was frightened and couldn't believe her eyes; she had never
dreamed of such a celebration, and she hung on Jim's arm.
Then, as women on men's shoulders began to emerge riding
high above the crowd, she climbed onto Jim's.'

Soon two men, noticing Odile, came over and introduced themselves
and offered to carry her. One is described as a Russian prince, the other
as an American. Odile's response to the kind offer was:

'Me glad have three biggest horses at ball and be able to change
when me like.'

The description of the ball in Chapter Eleven of *Jules et Jim* is
extremely entertaining. Suffice it to say, Odile had a wonderful night.
The American and the Russian had a hard job of protecting Odile's tiny
loincloth, preserving her modesty. When the beauty contest started,
Jules and Jim saw Odile waiting nervously and when her time came,
her naked body covered in talc, she emerged onto the balcony and

adopted the pose of Venus to rapturous shouts and ovations. When Lucie was worried about Odile, the men reassure her that Odile only does what she wants and that she's safe wherever she goes. Odile later went home with the Russian. Jim described feeling jealous but acknowledged that the nature of their relationship meant giving each other maximum freedom.[14]

Euphemia's experience of the 1908 Bal des Quat'z'Arts was that she went with Roché and Hessel but spent time in the company of Maresco Pearce, an English artist, and the Russian Prince George.

Duncan Grant had attended the ball the previous year when the theme had been 'Orientalism'. He remembered that the general effect was like some gigantic Eastern bazaar, or a slave market. There was a lot of exposed flesh. He wrote to Lytton:

'I have just seen lust walking about undisguised, debauchery carried to its limits, drunkenness and frenzy everywhere prevalent… Everyone was exceedingly good natured and uproarious; the champagne was unlimited so that being fairly drunk I was able to stand the shocks I might not otherwise have been able to hold. As a spectacle it was unrivalled.'[15]

In Franz Hessel's novella *Romance Parisienne* which was published in 1920, he writes four letters to Roché ostensibly from the Front in the First World War, reminiscing on their time together in Paris before the war. The character of Pamela (based on Euphemia) appears in the final two letters. It is a simultaneous account of the same period Roché writes about in 1907. Hessel's girlfriend known as Lucie in *Jules et Jim* is referred to now as Lotte. This scene describes Pamela's first glimpse of Lotte, who Hessel had initially been trying to keep secret from her:

'But when she saw Lotte, she knelt before her, and pressed in her curious French-English patois to finally make her acquaintance. With this, the great black and colourful Indian

---

14. Henri-Pierre Roché, *Jules et Jim*, 1953, chapters 8–11.
15. Duncan Grant, letter to Lytton Strachey, 20 May 1906, British Library.

shawl she now wears instead of a coat, fell off her shoulder. Underneath was revealed not the cowl-like house dress that we had loved on her, but an elegant afternoon gown. At my astonished gaze she informed me, "Oh my dear Madman (she called me nothing else), you see me all elegant. The terrible times are over, I am once again going out only with rich Russian princes and Americans."'

She described feeling uncomfortable in her new elegant gown and unclips some hooks and eyes:

'… until the whole dress sprang off and her wonderful milk white shoulders showed through. "Me voila" she called with flashing eyes and all three of us laughed heartily. "You must come to mine," said Pamela, "I have to show you my new clothes." She led us not into some elegant apartment, but into her old home in the mews house on the other side of the churchyard. It was still the same bald room. On the mantel lived the same dolls…The bed, a large double mattress without anything underneath it, looked like dear misery. A piano stood very unplayed in a corner, all that her husband had left her. Her many new silk dresses hung in a splendid wardrobe.'

As it was evening, Pamela insisted they stay for food and cooked them pork cutlets with rice and tomatoes, followed by a foam omelette.

'On this evening a great friendship began between Pamela and Lotte. The beautiful English woman took the astonished and thrill-seeking child on all her wild travels. But she guarded it jealously and sent all admirers away when she wanted to be alone with Lotte. I had a sad time.'

The implication is that Pamela uses her charms to seduce Lotte. Roché's diaries confirm that Euphemia had expressed an interest in sleeping with Hessel's girlfriend Giselle.

Roché described the first meeting of Euphemia and Giselle (Odile and Lucie) in *Jules et Jim*:

> 'The occasion took place in a cosmopolitan patisserie. Odile talked about her excellent but interrupted education and behaved herself alternately as an exotic princess and a street child. Lucie left her the initiative and Odile made full use of it. Her face was aristocratic and her voice showed breeding, but her facial expressions were crude; she was like Hogarth's Shrimp Girl, whereas Lucie might have been one of Goethe's grand-daughters.'

Female Lovers

Sapphism and sapphic sex are mentioned by Vanessa Stephen in relation to her visit from Nina after her first trip to Paris in 1906. The next mention is on the trip to Holland in August 1907 with Roché and Hessel, when Hessel is pretending to prefer men and Euphemia tells him she would like to 'taste women' and that she might try it one of these days. After Euphemia returned to Paris from Holland, her first letter to Roché in September 1907 said 'Me no kiss cocottes'. But when Euphemia denied something in a letter, often the reverse was true. There is no doubt that in the period of instability in the autumn of 1907 when she was developing her career as a café star, there had been some dancing with other beautiful cocottes and probably much more. When she met Hessel and Roche's German lover Giselle, she stated that she would like to sleep with her, and this is confirmed in Hessel's description of Ofe wanting an exclusive relationship with Lucy around the time of the Bal des Quat'z'Arts. At the 1908 ball, Euphemia performed a lesbian dance on stage with the Empress, the highest-ranking cocotte at the ball.

One of her lovers from that evening, Maresco Pearce, wrote in his diary:

'Euphemia was back in London and one day turned up with a French girl named Audre – I don't remember ever hearing her surname, if she ever had one. She was a queer girl – incredibly casual in her way of life and in her get up for that matter, even more so than Euphemia. She lived in Montparnasse and frequented the Dome, where I had seen her but now met her for the first time. I last saw her in the autumn of 1913 and she was living with Hener [James] Skene [Isadora Duncan's pianist]. She was intelligent and amusing; on this occasion in my studio she quoted an entire poem of Baudelaire, which naturally appealed to me.'[16]

Euphemia soon became embroiled in another scandalous love triangle. The main protagonist requires a chapter to himself; the cynical and jaundiced Wyndham Lewis called him the High Priest of Elemental Passion, alias The Crow:

'He is a spotty-waistcoated, cockney voiced little shit, with a truculent journalistic attitude in life, just the sort of boy the girls like. He was coy and indulged in the luxury of calling me names… I would take it out of his dirty carcass only a "High Priest Assaulted" would be a good name.'

This was Euphemia's next lover; Aleister Crowley.

16. Maresco Pearce, *Reminiscences*, diary for 1911, p. 33, Tate Archives.

EIGHT

The Master of the Dark Arts – Aleister Crowley

*Sometimes she's brutal
and savage and treacherous.*
– Henri-Pierre Roché

ALEISTER CROWLEY WAS AN ENGLISH OCCULTIST, philosopher, ceremonial magician, poet, painter and novelist. He was three years older than Euphemia. In 1898 he joined the Hermetic Order of the Golden Dawn, where he trained in ceremonial magic. He was a great mountaineer; he climbed peaks in Mexico and attempted the first ascent (unsuccessfully) of K2. In 1904 he married Rose Kelly (sister of the well-known portrait artist Gerald Kelly) and whilst on honeymoon in Cairo he wrote *The Book of the Law*, a sacred text which served as the basis for the religion he founded, Thelema. He identified himself as the prophet entrusted with guiding humanity into the Aeon of Horus. He was bisexual and believed that spiritual ecstasy could be achieved through sexual ecstasy and sodomy. Rose was an alcoholic, who lived in London with their daughter. Crowley arrived in Paris in January 1908, staying at rue Vavin. He quickly became a regular at the Café du Dome and made the acquaintance of Augustus John, Wyndham Lewis and Euphemia. He and Euphemia became lovers.

In June 1908, once the University of Cambridge summer term had ended, Crowley's young lover and acolyte, Victor Neuburg, joined him in Paris. Victor was attracted to Euphemia. Crowley decided to recruit Euphemia into playing a practical joke on Victor. He encouraged Euphemia to flirt with Victor and encouraged him to fall in love with her; this she did. Victor became infatuated with her and they announced their engagement (Victor being unaware of her married status). Aleister Crowley then took it upon himself to convince Victor,

Photograph of Aleister Crowley, *c.* 1908

who had hitherto only engaged in homosexual sex, that he would need to be practised in the art of pleasuring a woman and so he took him to a brothel in Paris where Victor was initiated in the art of heterosexual sex. Victor now felt uneasy that he had betrayed Euphemia by having slept with another woman and Crowley encouraged him to confess to Euphemia what he had done. Euphemia pretended to be outraged, called off the engagement and Victor was in despair. It was then revealed to Victor that in fact Aleister and Euphemia were a couple and the whole charade had just been a test of his suitability to be a disciple for Crowley. Victor was stunned, disturbed and devastated by this experience.

Crowley was Neuburg's master and asked him to follow his instructions. Neuburg had proved his fidelity to Crowley. Later, they went to North Africa where they performed a bizarre set of rituals. The sexual relationship was intense and the rituals required great courage and daring as they combined sex and magic. They were based on the occult rituals of the Enochian system of Dr John Dee.

Aleister Crowley was a complex character. He enjoyed sado-masochistic sex and as his relationship with Neuburg suggests, he also

Augustus John, *Euphemia Lamb*, pencil on paper, 34 x 17 cm

enjoyed manipulating and humiliating people. However, Euphemia was taken with him; she was unafraid of his darkness and corrupting influences. She stayed in his life as a friend, although she wrote to Roché that she 'hated him' and experienced shame at the thought of what they had done together. In September 1908, on her return to England, Euphemia wrote to Crowley. This letter inspired him to write his poem 'Telepathy' about her and her part in the Neuburg initiation (see Appendix B). Crowley also immortalised Euphemia in a poem called 'After Judgment' (see Appendix B) and in his collection, *The Winged Beetle*, he calls her 'Dorothy'. 'After Judgment' is an ode to love and their sex life; after Aleister left Paris he went to North Africa with Victor Neuburg. Euphemia stayed in touch with Crowley, and her second husband Ned Grove was a Crowley acolyte.

Aleister Crowley was one of the icons of the twentieth century. He had a huge revival during the acid culture of the 1960s; his esoteric folklore and magical practices were worshipped by contemporary music artists such as The Beatles (his image appears on the cover of *Sgt Pepper's Lonely Hearts Club Band*), The Rolling Stones and Led Zeppelin. He was known as 'The Beast'. His biographer Martin Booth describes him as 'self-confident, brash, eccentric, egotistic, highly intelligent, arrogant, witty, wealthy and when it suited him cruel'.

Was Euphemia a femme fatale? Her love affairs were in the main mutually advantageous and not harmful. She conspired to use her charms to ensnare Victor Neuburg into a trap and it does seem to be an occasion when the term can be applied

Photograph of Aleister Crowley, Golden Dawn, 1910

to her. Euphemia was attracted to the finer qualities of Crowley, his intelligence and his sheer force of personality, and seems to have overlooked his more despicable traits. We know that on her return to England she felt shame for her part in this affair. In his autobiography, *Confessions*, Crowley said that Euphemia was 'incomparably beautiful; Augustus John had painted her again and again and no more exquisite loveliness has ever adorned any canvas… She had a husband around the corner, but one ignores such flim flam in Montparnasse.' He described her as incapable of love and was at first resentful of her lack of emotional connection, but he came to admire her ability to satisfy herself sexually without personalising the attraction with the idea of love:

> 'She was capable of simulating the greatest extravagances of passion. Indeed the transports were genuine enough; but they were carefully isolated from the rest of life, so that she was in no way compromised by them. At the time I rather resented this; I was inclined to call her shallow and even to feel somewhat insulted; but now I see that she was in reality acting like an adept, keeping the planes well apart. She was an extremely good friend, though she never allowed her friendship to interfere with her interest.
>
> 'She was in addition, one of the best companions that a man could possibly have. Without pretence of being a blue stocking, she could hold her own in any conversation about art, literature or music. She was the very soul of gaiety, and an incomparable comedienne. One of my most delightful memories is the matching of our wits. It was rapture to compete with her in what we called "leg-pulling", which may be defined as inducing someone to make a fool of himself.'

During the initiation of Victor Neuburg in the desert in Algeria in December 1909, Crowley supposedly changed his appearance and became a 'beautiful courtesan' called Euphemia, and tempted Neuburg to leave his protective circle to come and make love to her.

In the 1920s Aleister Crowley founded the Abbey of Thelema, a small house in Cefalù, Sicily, which he used as a temple and spiritual centre. A contemporary of Euphemia, an artist's model called Betty May and her husband Raoul Loveday, a worshipper of Crowley, visited the Abbey. Raoul died of typhoid after conducting a blood sacrifice ritual. Betty May wrote a chapter in her autobiography *Tiger Woman*, dealing with this tragedy, called 'The Mystic'. Betty May described the Mystic thus:

> 'He had dark glowing, hypnotic eyes and loose sallow skin, with very full red lips. He had a massive head, on which was placed a glossy, black curly wig. I discovered that his head was shaved.'

Before they travelled to Sicily, Raoul came under the spell of Crowley in his temporary temple in Holland Park. Betty May wrote of how Raoul was brought into the Thelemite cult with drug-taking, and how he visited every day and often didn't return for several nights. One of the people she turned to during this difficult period was Euphemia:

> 'One of the people who was very kind to me during this awful period was Euphemia Lamb, and I can never be grateful enough to her for it. I was in despair.'

Jacob Epstein and his wife Peggy also helped Betty in trying to get Raoul out of Crowley's grip, but failed. After Raoul's death and the publication of her autobiography, Crowley sued Betty May for libel and lost his court case.

Towards the end of her time in Paris, Euphemia's letters to Roché became increasingly desperate. The letters give us a fascinating insight into her life, her state of mind and her struggles. When Roché was travelling, they tended to be pleas for his return and she often mentions other men to make him jealous; in her denial of her sex life and her repeated assertion that she is a virgin, there is an inference that the reverse is the case. Frequently the letters detail her thinking she was pregnant and appealing for money for an abortion; it is difficult to know whether they are genuine or to read them more cynically. Roché summarised that there were two fixed themes in her letters; the legend of the child (pregnancy) and her desire to come and join him in Germany. There were also many requests for money, some of which he satisfied. Whilst staying at Semenov's family home in the Black Forest, Roché and Semenov did invite Euphemia to come on a walking tour with them. But in August 1908 Euphemia announced that with her debts paid and there being no baby, she was going to return to England.

Euphemia was keen to leave the café cocotte life behind her, and so a plan was hatched with the help of Henry Lamb and a friend called Wallie. Euphemia travelled to England via a short holiday in Brittany with the two men.

William Orpen, *The Draughtsman and His Model*, c. 1900s, watercolour, 43.8 x 61.3 cm

NINE

Return to London – *Moi Toujours Lady Ici*

Had it not been for her excessive casualness in treating men, she could almost have passed for a lady. – Henri-Pierre Roché

BY 19TH AUGUST, Euphemia was writing to Roché from Hermanville-sur-Mer, where she was on holiday with Lamb and Wallie. She wrote:

> 'I have a very big room with a great big quaint bed in it. Harry [Lamb] has a room near mine very much bigger but not as nice as mine. Wallie has a little cottage close by. It is much nicer than Holland. We are the only people here and the peasants are very friendly and stare at us.'

They stayed in Brittany for about a week, then returned home on the ferry:

> 'I had a very bad crossing, the boat rolled and tossed the whole night it was impossible to lie down as I kept being thrown to the floor. Luckily I travelled first class so there was only one other lady besides myself in the salon and as neither of us was sick this made things a little better.'

The return to England marked a transition for Euphemia; from being a café cocotte to becoming a lady.

Within a week of her return, she was sitting for Jacob Epstein who was modelling a bust of her. She wrote to Roché:

William Orpen, *The Bather*, *c.* 1908, watercolour

'I love London at night. I go all over it on top of a bus and watch the people and the lights.'

She also wrote that she had some regrets:

'Now when I think of my life in Paris I hate it. I hate all the men.'[1]

and

'Quand moi voir Dome and everything moi shame and triste dans ma ventre [belly]. Je crois I was tout a fait imbecile a Paris.'

Euphemia stayed initially with Augustus John at 131 Cheyne Walk.[2] John wrote to Lamb:

1. Euphemia Lamb, letter to Henri–Pierre Roché, 9 September 1908, Harry Ransom Center, Univ. of Texas.
2. Her letters to Roché in September 1908 have a Cheyne Walk address.

Jacob Epstein, *First Bust of Euphemia Lamb*, 1908, bronze, 37.5 × 40 × 20.3 cm

'Lobelia occupies Epstein's room – he having gone to Paris.'[3]

John also suggested that Euphemia was keen on the idea of running a restaurant, 'but I doubt she's not too much of the putain to carry it off'. This idea came to nothing and Euphemia moved into a house at 14 Whitehead's Grove in Chelsea, bought for her by her friend, Morton Sands. Sands was a wealthy American art collector; he and his sister Ethel Sands, an artist, were the major collectors of the work of Walter Sickert during his lifetime. Sickert started the Camden Town Group in 1911, its original members included Augustus John, Henry Lamb, James Dickson Innes and Wyndham Lewis.

Maresco Pearce records in his diary details of Euphemia's life during this time:

'Euphemia was living in Whitehead's Grove that autumn in a house in which she had been installed by Morton Sands, who

3. Augustus John, letter to Henry Lamb, September 1908, TAM 15B 39/52.

was still her official "owner" – is that the right term or is it "master"? for she was after all his official mistress.'[4]

As well as the modelling for Epstein, Augustus John wanted Euphemia to model for a huge painting he was planning, entitled *Lyric Fantasy*. This painting was to include John's dead wife Ida, as well as his current mistress Dorelia. The fantasy was to resurrect the women he had loved and admired, together with the children. A lyric fantasy is a dream of a golden age and the restored plenitude of the maternal body. John poured his grief and his mourning for Ida into this psychic space and produced a consoling gypsy arcadia. It is a frieze depicting women and children, a symbolist allegory on the various stages of a woman's life: dancing girl, mother and mistress.

Augustus John, *Lyric Fantasy*, c. 1913–14, oil paint and graphite on canvas, 238 x 472 cm

Augustus John painted Euphemia again in *The Way Down to the Sea* in the winter of 1908/9.

Euphemia knew Percy Wyndham Lewis, a good friend of Augustus John, from the Café du Dome. She became even better acquainted with him when he became her neighbour, moving to 14B Whitehead's Grove in 1908. Lewis had felt so in awe of John that it inhibited his ability to

4. Maresco Pearce, diary, 1910, Tate Archives, p. 22.

Augustus John, *Wyndham Lewis (1882–1957)*, c. 1905, oil

think of himself as a great artist, although history would now suggest that Lewis made the greater contribution to art as both an artist and writer. Lewis's return to London marked the beginning of his career as a writer when he published his first article in *The English Review*. For Wyndham Lewis, art was the only meaningful tool for describing the condition of the world. Having been expelled from the Slade he went to Paris aged eighteen to begin his intellectual journey. He was an outsider, an opponent and an innovator. He would often be wearing a black cape, with his back to the wall and discoursing his opinions and ideas. He later wrote fierce satirical attacks on the class system and the

Bloomsbury Group. He despised authors who catered for the degraded public taste for sentiment and romance for money.

Lewis was working on his novel *Tarr* when he lived next door to Euphemia. Lewis and Euphemia had read Dostoevsky novels in French whilst in Paris and were both great admirers of his works. Lewis used a Dostoevskian sensibility and psychology in *Tarr*:

> 'It is probably Dostoevskian only in the intricacy of the analysis of character and motive, and a comprehension of that never failing paradox, the real, in contrast with the monotonous self-consistency of what man invents without reference to nature, in pursuit of the ideal.'[5]

In *Tarr*, Lewis created the memorable character of Anastasya, a woman associated with the avant-garde as a consort; she is the embodiment of the newly emergent twentieth-century woman:

> 'There was an explosion of excitement; Anastasya appeared. She came out of that social flutter astonishingly inapposite, like a mask come to life. The little fanfare of welcome continued. She was much more outrageous than Kreisler could ever hope to be, bespangled and accoutred like a bastard princess or aristocratic concubine of the household of Peter the Great.' (From a scene at a party, *Tarr*, p. 114.)

Anastasya is a fiercely intelligent and utterly unsentimental character. She and Tarr (based on Lewis himself) talk headily about art, sex and life. The protagonist in *Tarr* says that 'Surrender to a woman was a sort of suicide for an artist.' In his mind, women were the death of art. Lewis argued that the creative man should be above the Philistine populace and above sexual appetite. Lewis's friend, Sturge Moore, had warned him against any woman who used the 'slop of sex' to trap him. 'If a man puts his genius between her legs she will cover it with any petticoat and

5. Wyndham Lewis, *Rude Assignment*, 1950, p. 152.

no one will see it again.' Lewis was paranoid that a woman might have the power to enfeeble a man and tame his genius. Lewis had seen this happen with John, who had succumbed to a family romance that had affected his genius.

Wyndham Lewis greatly disliked Dorelia. He was keen for her to go off with Henry Lamb, as he thought that would stop her muzzling John's genius. Lewis writes of Dorelia as the 'sickening bitch he [John] has attached himself to'.

Given that Lewis had known Euphemia in her wild days in Paris and then ended up being her next-door neighbour in Chelsea, one wonders whether he hadn't observed some of her antics for the character of Anastasya. Euphemia thought Wyndham Lewis was a brilliant thinker; she is quoted as saying he was so 'brilliant, it isn't a wonder it comes out of his skin in spots!'

Later in 1909 there was an argument between Lewis and John from which it became apparent that Lewis had quarrelled with several people John held in high regard. The personalities and circumstances are detailed in three rambling reconciliatory letters between the two. It seems Euphemia was responsible for some of the unpleasantness. She accused Lewis of boasting in a letter that she had made love to him and that she had been laying loud claims to a bill for several meals he was supposed to owe her. Lewis had also quarrelled with her husband, Henry Lamb. Lewis told John, 'Lamb is one of the elements out of which your entanglement with me has grown.' The argument may also have been about money. Generally, John was a very forgiving man, Euphemia a generous woman and Wyndham Lewis a man who set store by making himself the enemy in most situations. He was against most things; presumably he was jealous of Henry Lamb's close relationship with John.

There is some suggestion from a letter that Augustus John wrote to Dorelia that Euphemia had indeed slept with Wyndham Lewis. He wrote:

'Lobelia had six men in her room last night, representing six European powers and all silent as the grave as I had an intense desire to kick all their European arses. I left Lobelia publicly expressing a wish to nest with me tonight. I gave her my last address to call on – by way of protest. [Wyndham] Lewis becomes intolerably bilious now and then… I seem to detect a certain faiblesse [feeble] perfunctoriness or incertitude in the reasoning powers he piques himself on. However, Lobelia calls him a "neuter" which perhaps explains all. I according to the same authority am a "frother".

Euphemia continued to see Henry Lamb when he was in London; they repaired to his cottage in Wiltshire in the spring of 1909 and he painted this intimate and languid portrait of Euphemia in repose.

Henry Lamb, *Portrait of Euphemia Lamb*, *c.* 1909, watercolour

Ambrose McEvoy, *Euphemia Lamb (The Ferry)*, 1909, oil on canvas, 48.3 x 73 cm

In May 1909 Euphemia was the model for an oil painting by Ambrose McEvoy called *The Ferry*. The painting was large and later cut in half to make two paintings; the family scene in the boat and a separate portrait of Euphemia in a red velvet dress. He depicts Euphemia as fey, wide-eyed and innocent, yet she is plucking the petals off a flower in the painting, an allusion to her sexual freedom. The painting was exhibited along with Augustus John's *The Way Down to the Sea* at the New English Art Club Summer Exhibition in 1909. McEvoy became a celebrated portrait painter; he had been at

Jacob Epstein, *Second Portrait of Euphemia Lamb*, 1911, bronze, H: 52.5 cm

the Slade School of Art with Augustus John and William Orpen and was part of their bohemian set.

This period in Chelsea was one of regular work for Euphemia. Her finances improved, her house was provided for her and she was becoming increasingly respectable. The transition from café cocotte to English lady was becoming a reality. She had brought her fine Parisienne clothes over with her and she started to frequent the Café Royal. The bohemian artists, although still largely living and working in Bloomsbury and Chelsea, made the Café Royal in Regent Street the headquarters of their social scene. In 1911, Euphemia sat again for Jacob Epstein and he produced a second bust of her head. Euphemia enjoyed the high life and meeting the cognoscenti and aristocracy at the Café Royal, but she was still drawn to bohemia. Her next lover was a true bohemian: the Welsh artist James Dickson Innes.

TEN

James Dickson Innes – A True Bohemian

Her clear enamel eyes and radiant complexion.
She frolicked like a young dog and drank too much.
– Henri-Pierre Roché

JAMES DICKSON INNES was a Welsh artist, born in 1887, the same year as Euphemia, and a true bohemian. Innes shared a studio with Henry Lamb and Augustus John at 8 Fitzroy Street and exhibited at the Friday Club in 1908 at the home of Vanessa and Clive Bell (46 Gordon Square) whilst he was a third-year student at the Slade. That summer he travelled to the South of France with John Fothergill. The weather was poor, so they ventured further south to Collioure where Matisse and Derain had painted a few years previously. Here, Innes produced some fine landscape watercolours. Euphemia moved to Cheyne Walk in the autumn of 1908; on Innes' return from France, he and fellow artist Derwent Lees moved to lodgings at 125 Cheyne Walk, so they would have been neighbours. According to Randolph Schwabe, Innes was a man of great personal charm, and his zest for life and for romantic adventure was immense. He had been a promising student at the Slade. However, he was diagnosed with tuberculosis on his return from France in 1908. His mother became very involved in trying to save her son and they spent a great deal of time together finding convalescent cures. The return from France also brought him into contact with Euphemia and he became infatuated with her.

In January 1909, whilst convalescing with his mother in St Ives, he wrote to his friend John Fothergill:

'I have written a new poem on Euphemia,
    Euphe had a little lamb.
    With hair of brightest gold

Euphe lost her little lamb
For the little lamb grew old.
And he became a dirty ram
Euphemia then grew cold.

Euphe seeks another lamb
And sees one albeit bold
She said "In here you'd better jam"
So now I do not care a dam.
My story having told.'

Augustus John described Innes thus:

'He cut quite an arresting figure; a Quaker hat, a coloured silk scarf and a long black overcoat, set off features of a slightly cadaverous cast, with glittering black eyes, a wide sardonic mouth, a prominent nose and a large bony forehead, invaded by streaks of thin black hair. He carried an ebony cane with a gold top and spoke with a heavy English accent.'

Innes moved to Paris in 1909 and befriended the artist Matthew Smith. Innes' trip to Paris transformed his life. The two of them visited Gertrude Stein's salon and saw paintings by Matisse for the first time. Innes rented a studio in Montparnasse and produced the studio painting titled *The Bead Chain*. The features of the girl in this painting resemble Euphemia, although she is modelled on a photo of an Algerian dancer. In Paris he met Euphemia again in a café. We know she had been in his thoughts and letters for at least a year and now he declared his love and Euphemia reciprocated. Euphemia was his model for his next studio painting, *Girl Playing a Guitar*, and the influence of Matisse's decorative patterns can be seen in this artwork. The relationship with Euphemia enabled him to move out of the convalescent cocoon his mother had been trying to wrap him up in to preserve his health. As with Henry Lamb four years earlier, Euphemia catalysed Innes' adventurous spirit and she may have been responsible

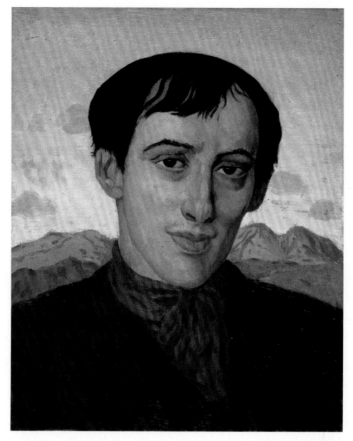

Ian Strang, *James Dickson Innes (1887–1914)*, 1913, oil on panel, 40.5 x 32.6 cm

for his renewed energy and confidence as a painter during this period.

Innes set out with Euphemia for Collioure once again in May 1910. Euphemia was the 'lady of his dreams' according to Augustus John. In the words of John Rothenstein:

'They met in a Paris café and Innes at once responded to the beauty of her pale oval face, classical in feature yet animated by a spirit, passionate, reckless and witty, and the heavy honey-hued hair.'[1]

1. John Rothenstein, *Modern English Painters*, 1956.

Left: James Dickson Innes, *The Bead Chain*, 1910, oil on canvas
Right: James Dickson Innes, *Girl with a Guitar*, c. 1910, oil on canvas, 157.5 x 114.3 cm

The evidence for Euphemia going to Collioure with Innes is in a letter that John Fothergill wrote to Albert Rutherstone:

> '[Derwent] Lees tells me strange things about Innes – in short
> – Lamb off (sounds like 11 o'clock pm in a nasty eating house)
> and also his allowance from his mother – gone to Paris.'

This cryptic message suggests that they returned to Paris, possibly separately. When later asked about the trip to Collioure with Innes by Winifred Coombe Tennant, Euphemia did not deny it, and two of the watercolours suggest she was there.

By the late summer of 1910, Innes was in North Wales visiting his aunt in Penmaenmawr. During this holiday he saw Arenig Fawr for the first time, a twin-peaked summit over 2,900 feet high; it caught his imagination and he had to paint it. He stayed at a small inn at Rhyd y Fen at the foot of the mountain. When Innes returned to London in November, he reconnected with Euphemia. Their relationship was passionate but not exclusive. She was still living in Chelsea with

James Dickson Innes, *Euphemia Lamb standing on a Rock*, c. 1911, watercolour

her friend Morton Sands. Innes gave Euphemia a number of the watercolours from Wales which she was to sell for him, so in effect she was acting as his dealer. Maresco Pearce wrote in his diary:

'One evening I went there [Whitehead's Grove] after leaving the studio and she showed me a number of watercolours that Innes had made in Wales that summer and had left with her. I was astonished at their beauty and at the sudden change to his natural manner. Up til then I had not been much interested in his work. These Welsh watercolours, on the contrary, have come off with a vengeance. They were exceedingly original, though some of them I thought, showed the influence of Hokusai. Euphemia said he had left them with her to sell for him.'[2]

At this time Augustus John was showing at the Chenil Gallery a series of small oils painted on wooden panels which he had completed in the South of France. They captured the fresh, Fauve-like, plein air landscapes and captivated Innes. They gave him the idea to invite John to Arenig. Innes' January 1911 show of his watercolours was a critical and commercial success. In March 1911, Innes returned to Rhyd y Fen, this time armed with wooden panels and oil paints. Augustus John came to join him; he was thirty-three years old, successful, wealthy and famous, and he was curious to see what his fellow Welshman and apprentice was up to. John wrote to Dorelia:

'This is the most wonderful place I've seen. The air is superb and the mountains are wonderful.'

He spoke about how he felt full of work and felt that the two of them had found 'the reflection of some miraculous promised land'.

Augustus John was a gypsy at heart and during his tenure at Liverpool University art school in 1902 had met John Sampson, the librarian there but also a Professor of Philology who compiled the Welsh-Romany language dictionary. He was a mentor to John and taught him the Romany language. John emulated this lifestyle and enjoyed taking a gypsy caravan out on the road. Sampson had a house 15 miles away from Arenig at Betws Gwerfil Goch and the two of them paid him a visit. Sampson's visitors' book bears their signatures for 12 March 1911.

Innes and John painted various views of the mountain and the surrounding countryside. John said of Innes:

'He was never happier than when painting in this area.'

---

2. Maresco Pearce, diary, Tate Archive, p. 22.

Augustus John, *The Girl in the Green Dress*, *c.* 1911, watercolour

They decided to extend their stay and found a cottage at Nant Ddu, a mile away, at a rent of £10 per year:

> 'At last Innes discovered a cottage which we decided to take. It stood a few miles from the Inn by the brook called Nant Ddu and looked out on Arenig. We furnished it sparsely and returned in the following year and yet again.'

Euphemia and Dorelia came to stay with them at the cottage. Innes and John set up their easels side by side and the master/pupil relationship was reversed, Innes teaching John how to tackle landscape and colour. John was teaching Innes to paint in oils. John's *Llyn Tryweryn* is one of his greatest works and was produced here. Innes was painting prolifically, and the Japanese print motif can be seen to influence the cloud formations hovering above the mountains. John thought that Innes' feverish and possessive attachment to the mountain reflected his strong feelings towards Euphemia – and how the two

Left: James Dickson Innes, *Girl Standing by a Lake*, 1911–1912, oil on panel, 38.1 x 29.2 cm
Right: James Dickson Innes, *The Girl in the Cottage, c.* 1911, oil on panel, 32 x 22 cm

were merging together in a consummation of painting and passion. John said he thought that in Innes' mind, Arenig Fawr and Euphemia were interchangeable. Innes painted Euphemia in this landscape many times. He asked her to stand for him in front of Arenig Fawr, amongst the boulders of the stream and on the shore of Llyn Tryweryn. He also painted her inside the cottage seated at a dressing table, and we can see that the artists had decorated the interior walls with a bright pink and blue fresco.

These paintings were so successful that they were included in the Armory Show in New York in 1913. John had thirty-eight paintings in the exhibition and Innes had six. Euphemia appeared as a model in some of Innes' landscapes, as well as being the subject of an Epstein bust at the show.

During their time in Wales, Augustus John had invited his old friend from Liverpool, the artist Albert Lipczinski, to visit Arenig and make use of the cottage. When Lipczinski and his wife arrived, they were expecting it to be empty but Innes and Euphemia were still in residence. Lipczinski telegrammed his disappointment to John, who replied, 'Get the Bastards out.' It seemed that the two couples managed

James Dickson Innes, *Landscape with a Figure, Arenig, c.* 1911, oil on board, 20.9 x 31.2 cm

to co-exist and one can definitely see Innes' artistic influence on Lipczinski's landscapes of the surrounding valleys and mountains.

John said of Innes, 'By the intensity of his vision and his passionately romantic outlook, his work will live.' However, Innes' life was finely balanced on a line between his creative impulse and the prospect of self-destruction. The underbelly of bohemia is excess; Elizabeth Wilson argues in her book *The Bohemians: The Glamorous Outcasts* (2000) that:

> 'If Bohemia was a journey as well as a destination, it was a journey into the dark to a land of danger as well as pleasure. It promised a path along the edge of a precipice and it was impossible to know in advance whether that path led to revelation or madness, triumph or madness.'

In September 1911, Euphemia was at the Café Royal with Innes and Augustus John, who was entertaining John Quinn. Quinn was an American collector and a patron of John, Innes and Epstein. At this time, with Dorelia in the countryside with the children, Augustus John had embarked on an ill-fated affair with Frida Strindberg, the former wife of the Swedish dramatist, August Strindberg. When he attempted to end the affair, she threatened suicide on several occasions. Quinn recorded in his diary:

'Mme Strindberg had taken poison and the doctor said she would not last the night. This damned Austrian woman has wasted John's time – upset his nerves – played hell with his work...'

Quinn described how one afternoon during his visit, Innes arrived, 'His black hair flat over his forehead, his face very pale, his teeth missing, wearing a dark green tie and a big black felt hat.' John was present and concerned about the situation with Frida Strindberg, Quinn suggested that John join him on his trip to France to evade Frida. John invited Euphemia and another artist's model, Lillian Shelley, to accompany them to France and the girls agreed. He bought four tickets for the crossing the next morning. The group of them went back to John's studio and partied. Quinn recorded:

'All drunk and John sang and acted wonderfully. Two divans full – Lillian the best natured.'

However, at Charing Cross Station the next morning, Euphemia and Lillian didn't turn up. Instead, on the platform Frida Strindberg greeted Quinn and John with a revolver. With a tussle, they managed to board the train without her, although she caught up with them at the boat.

All six of the Innes paintings at the Armory Show in 1913 were loaned by Quinn. Quinn's diary also records lunch with Winston Churchill at the Ritz during that visit.

Innes was dicing with death; his creativity the outcome of knowing he was not going to live long. Innes' tuberculosis was progressive; his health meant that he travelled to Morocco and back to his parents in Tavistock to convalesce. In 1914 he was admitted to a nursing home in Swanley, Kent. Augustus John took Euphemia to visit him one last time. 'The meeting of these two was painful – we left them alone together. It was the last time I saw him.' Innes died on 22 August 1914, aged just twenty-seven.

Touchingly, even though Euphemia had moved on to another lover by the time of Innes' death, she spent the rest of her life buying back and collecting his art until she had the largest private collection. In 1923, there was an Innes Memorial Exhibition at the Tate, organised by Augustus John; Howard de Walden and Horace de Vere Cole both lent several paintings, but Euphemia supplied the most. She valued true artistic integrity, and the devotion and sacrifice of artists to their art. In Innes she had found a true bohemian who would not let life get in the way of his art. Perhaps because he knew he was dying, he lived at a greater intensity, but she was at his side on this journey which produced some of the best British art of the early twentieth century.

After the Second World War, the Welsh art collector Winifred Coombe Tennant developed an interest in Innes and John, and the art they had produced in Wales before the First World War. She also became interested in the women who were close to these young men, in particular Euphemia, intimate friend of Innes. In 1949, both Augustus John and Peter Harris had spoken to Winifred about Euphemia, who now lived in a house near Andover which was 'stacked with Innes drawings and paintings from floor to ceiling. Twenty-three dogs and many cats lived in it with her, her golden hair now bleached artificially, her blue eyes unchanged.'[3] In 1952 Winifred lent her two Innes watercolours to an exhibition of his work, shown with that of Kyffin Williams at the Leicester Galleries. Euphemia was among the other lenders. After the exhibition with the help of her friend Morton Sands, who acted as an intermediary, she was persuaded to sell the Innes watercolour *Cloud over Arenig* to Winifred:

'A most wonderful thing has happened today, the Innes I longed for, prayed for, came! Morton Sands brought it up from Euphemia's house in Hampshire – he came carrying it. "I have got your picture" he said.'

---

3. Peter Lord, *Winifred Coombe Tennant: A Life through Art*, 2007.

"How, how," I said "did you do this miracle?"

"By persuasion" he replied…

"It is very fine."[4]

A week later Morton Sands brought Euphemia herself to Cottesmore Gardens:

'I was resting in bed about 3.30pm… when the parlour-maid came in and said "Mrs Grove and Mr Morton Sands have called to see you." I rushed into a dressing gown and my lace cap and found them in the library. Euphemia, Innes' Euphemia, who walked in France with him – a tall, slender woman with a shock of golden hair, a pale complexion and lovely features. I could have fallen at her feet! I beheld her, the words came to me, "Ah did you once see Shelley plain." She was warmly friendly to me and begged me to come and see her. I showed her my large Innes of *Mountains in North Wales* and she exclaimed "It once belonged to me. I sold it to Lord Howard de Walden." I told her I knew it had been in his collection and that it was from there that the Leicester Galleries had bought it. She greatly admired the John drawing *Head of a woman* and the Condor drawing *Voyage of Plaisir a Dieppe*. She liked the Kyffin Williams and the Evan Walters – Morton Sands beaming with the success of our rencontre.'[5]

Winifred remained in touch with Euphemia. There is a telegram dated 1953 from Euphemia to Winifred: 'Your letter made me very happy would you like me to bring some pictures for you to see. Love Euphemia.'[6] In 1956, Winifred wrote to Euphemia after she had purchased an Innes painting at Christies, 'the sight of you would revive me'.[7]

---

4. Peter Lord, *Winifred Coombe Tennant: A Life through Art*, 2007.

5. Ibid.

6. Telegram at National Library of Wales Archives, Aberystwyth.

7. Peter Lord, *Winifred Coombe Tennant: A Life through Art*, 2007.

ELEVEN

The English Aristocrat and the Irish Poet

*No certainty. Chaos. Lovely things
and sudden disasters.* – Henri-Pierre Roché

BEFORE THE FIRST WORLD WAR, Euphemia had a house in Chelsea, and she was working as a café hostess at the Café Royal. She was still modelling for artists, but she had now set her sights on finding a husband despite the fact she was still married to Henry Lamb. She had seduced the richest man in England, Thomas Scott-Ellis, 8th Baron Howard de Walden who was friends with Augustus John and James Dickson Innes. Euphemia was friends with rich and powerful men. She was using Treasury Chambers-headed stationery to write to Roché during David Lloyd George's time there as Chancellor. Virginia Woolf placed Nina Lamb on the same sofa as Winston Churchill and John Quinn's diary had them all socialising together at the Ritz. In 1911 Euphemia frequented a new avant-garde nightclub set up by Frida Strindberg, the Cave of the Golden Calf, just off Regent Street. This low-ceilinged nightclub was decorated by Euphemia's friends, Wyndham Lewis and Jacob Epstein, and the club's motif was a phallic Golden Calf designed by Eric Gill as a symbol of biblical dissipation and idolatry.

In this palace of pleasure Euphemia met a young Englishman named Edmund Spencer Turton, who fell madly in love with her and described her as a 'ravishing creature'. Turton's father, Edmund Russborough Turton, was to be elected a Member of Parliament in 1915 and was created a baronet in 1926. He and his aristocratic family, who lived at Upsall Castle near Thirsk in Yorkshire, were not at all pleased with Turton's new friendship. They sent him to Argentina for a year in an attempt to break the relationship. Euphemia became ill and suffered some form of nervous breakdown, and his family paid for her to receive

Photograph of Edmund Spencer Turton, *c*. 1914

treatment in a Swiss sanatorium.

When Turton returned from Argentina they continued their romance and Euphemia became pregnant in December 1914. He rented for her the house of her dreams, Bedford House, which she had spied nine years previously on the banks of the river Thames in Chiswick Mall. He was renting the house from Arthur Sich, a member of the family who owned the Lamb brewery, who lived next door at Eynham House. At the outbreak of war Turton had joined his local regiment, the Yorkshire Hussars Yeomanry, in the rank of lieutenant and was sent to the Front. Although pregnant, Euphemia was still modelling for Augustus John. On 18 March 1915 John wrote to Euphemia asking her to visit his Mallard Street studio so that he could draw her portrait for the art connoisseur Louis Clarke, who wanted to obtain a drawing of her before he left for Belgrade.

The Turton family knew the Dickinson family and in 1914 Violet Dickinson had written to ask Virginia about Euphemia. Virginia responded:

> 'As to Nina Lamb, I think she is by this time a professional mistress. She has lived with various people. Last time I saw her she was in company with a little creature Adrian used to know – but heard the other day that she had taken a house at Hammersmith and was living with someone else. I believe she's rather nice and pretty – but without any morals.'[1]

1. Virginia Woolf, letter to Violet Dickinson, 27 April 1914, from *The Letters of Virginia Woolf 1912–1922*, Vol. 2, ed. by N. Nicolson.

Augustus John, *Portrait of Euphemia Lamb*, *c.*1907, graphite on white paper, 37 x 28 cm

Woolf continued:

'She began life in Manchester – her mother being apparently in the same line of life. She had a little money of her own, and she used to wander about London and Manchester (where a club was formed to protect her virtue) until she became Henry Lamb's mistress, and then his wife. They separated soon after that, and when we were in Paris a year or two afterwards she was a well known character.

'However I don't think she's wanting, and she certainly was amazingly pretty. I think she moves from person to person – I could write pages of her adventures, because she used to appear at intervals with amazing stories of her doings which were partly invented, but I think she was very attractive to a good many people.'[2]

Euphemia gave birth to a son, Edmund Christopher, whilst Turton was on leave from the Front. He returned to Belgium a couple of days after the birth and on 31 August 1915, was shot by a German sniper in a front line trench at Ypres and killed. He was twenty-six years old. The Turtons offered to bring up their grandson themselves or to pay for his upbringing and education whilst leaving him in the care of Euphemia. In the aftermath of Turton's death, Euphemia in her grief handed the baby over to his grandparents and entered into a passionate love affair with her Hammersmith neighbour and old friend Francis MacNamara.

Francis MacNamara

Francis was a poet, philosopher and hereditary heir to Doolin and Ennistymon in County Clare, Ireland. He had been educated at Harrow and Oxford and then lived for many years in the bohemian circle that centred around Augustus John. He was tall and fair with bright blue eyes. He had been best friends with Robert Gregory at

2. Ibid.

Gerald Brockhurst, *Francis MacNamara*, etching

Harrow, Lady Gregory's son, and through this connection knew W.B. Yeats. He was married with four children: the family lived a few hundred yards from Euphemia at nearby Hammersmith Terrace. He abandoned his wife of seven years, Yvonne, and their four young children. According to his daughter, Nicolette MacNamara (later Devas), the affair with Euphemia only lasted six months. After her time with Francis, Euphemia returned to London to reclaim her baby. Virginia Woolf was abreast of developments in the Turton/Lamb household. Woolf wrote to Duncan Grant:

> 'Nina has now taken away the baby. [The friend] knew Turton
> himself, who had only one fault – his chivalry; and he believed
> Nina to be the deserted wife of an officer who only wanted

a chance to reform, at least so she told the Dickinsons, just before he went to the Front.[3]

Euphemia moved her sister and her family permanently down from Manchester and installed them in Bedford House to look after the baby.

When Francis ran off with Euphemia, Yvonne and the children moved first to Chelsea to live with Nora and Gerald Summers, and then on to Alderney Manor (Augustus John's place near Poole), where they lived in a cottage. The MacNamara children grew up with the John children. Later they bought a house, Blashford, in the New Forest which was only a few miles away from the John's new residence at Fryern Court, and the two families continued to mingle.

Dorelia's sister, Edie McNeill, lived with the John family and helped raise the children. Francis would later marry Edie. It was not a happy marriage; Euphemia also became a frequent visitor at Fryern Court. Nicolette wrote in her memoir, *Two Flamboyant Fathers*:

'I was entranced by her exotic beauty and envied her bold confidence.'

She described Euphemia's voice as deep, hoarse and sexy. Euphemia instructed the teenage girls at Fryern in 'Mancraft'. Nicolette described how Euphemia 'lived for men', that this life appeared rewarding and how she remembered Euphemia throwing cast-off Schiaparelli dresses and other lovely clothes across the room for the girls to grab. She also kept £1 and £100 notes in her stockings and if she patted her thigh, the crackling noise would alert the girls to the fact that they might expect a tip.

In her memoir, Nicolette compared her real father, Francis, with Augustus John, her surrogate father:

'Augustus and Francis had certain characteristics in common. Both could be extravagantly gay in company with an overflow

3. Virginia Woolf, letter to Duncan Grant, from *The Letters of Virginia Woolf 1912–1922*, Vol. 2, ed. by N. Nicolson, p. 144.

of vitality – wit flashed like bullets in a Western, laughter exploded in manly roars, drink was drunk for the fun of getting drunk. Augustus was most attracted by a woman's beauty, while Francis was more interested in their character. They were young men, exceptionally handsome and talented, it was all very exuberant.'[4]

Francis's other daughter, Caitlin, remembered in her autobiography Euphemia coming to watch her in a dance show in Soho in the early 1930s. She also recalled how Euphemia made it her business to try and find Caitlin a husband:

'Various beer lords were suggested, but Ellen [Caitlin] was singularly lacking in the coquettish graces incumbent to tickle the jaded fancy of these gentlemen.'[5]

A few years later, Caitlin married the Welsh poet Dylan Thomas. Thomas' literary godfather was none other than Euphemia's former friend, Victor Neuburg.

After the Francis MacNamara affair, Euphemia returned to her life as a hostess and professional mistress at the Café Royal. Henry Lamb, writing in the 1920s, described the men that Euphemia consorted with as being 'rich and revolting'. We also have a description from Viva King about Euphemia during this period:

'I became very friendly with Euphemia Lamb, whom I had first met in Paris when I was a child… She came into my life during the war and father and I lunched with her at the Ritz. She was then always accompanied by a small, silent Russian Baron. In fact she was really a Bohemian, with the reedy instincts of a tart. She was not really beautiful but what was more important – she was fascinating. So many artists painted her repeatedly. It amused her to excite my hopes of a rich husband. One of

4. Nicolette Devas, *Two Flamboyant Fathers*, 1966, p. 27.
5. Caitlin MacNamara, *Story of a Woman*.

Dorothea St John George, *The Immortal Augustus at the Café Royal*, colour lithograph

the men she dangled was Louis Clark, the rich collector from Cambridge. I thought him too old and farty and anyway he was entirely enthralled by Euphemia.'[6]

Viva's account gives us a glimpse of Euphemia during her Café Royal years:

'She was too gay to be anyone's conception of a "femme fatale". She would squeal with delight when she saw a dish of meringues.'

---

6. Viva King, *The Weeping and The Laughter*, autobiography, p. 85.

Augustus John, *Older Euphemia in a Hat, c.* 1930, etching

Viva King accused Euphemia of stealing Augustus John's son, Romilly, from her, though the age gap between them would have been considerable.

Through Euphemia, Viva met Francis MacNamara. She was aware that they had been lovers and thought he was still in love with Euphemia. She described him as 'tall, fair and Irish and gay; witty and sympathetic one moment but then sulky and morose the next'.

Euphemia and Henry Lamb finally divorced in 1928. Euphemia continued to collect paintings by James Dickson Innes for the rest of her life. She remained great friends with Morton Sands and they would visit art exhibitions and country auctions together. She stayed in contact with Roché – there is a letter from Euphemia to him in 1931 trying to organise a rendezvous between the two of them in Paris. Euphemia kept in touch with Henry Lamb and Augustus John until her death. The Bloomsbury Group would have been constantly reminded of her because the Epstein garden statue, which Ottoline Morrell commissioned for the fountain at Garsington, was a near life-sized model of Euphemia. Euphemia was friends with Ralph and Frances Partridge who were part of the Bloomsbury set. But her days as a Bloomsbury muse were over.

Euphemia died on 26 January 1957 in hospital in Winchester, aged sixty-nine. Henry Lamb wrote a moving letter to her son:

'Having heard that Euphemia was very ill, I had wanted to write her a line of sympathy and an assurance of old but still living affection. I had no idea she was so very ill. I wish I could adequately offer you a word of condolence. But Euphemia was unique and I always feel grateful for the privilege of having been so closely associated with so much of her beauty and genius and glorious energy of character. I think I have never met anyone who knew her and who didn't feel those same things about her with admiration and gratitude. In this way I like to think something of her wonderful tonic influence is disseminated imperishably among us all.

Yours very sincerely,
Henry Lamb'
(dated 7 February 1957)

Henry Lamb died on 8 October 1960, aged seventy-seven. On his tombstone is inscribed: PAINTER, DOCTOR, MUSICIAN

Henry Lamb was a complex person; witty, intelligent, temperamental, cynical, perceptive, passionate and occasionally cruel. He was very attractive to both sexes and he fascinated and distressed his equally intelligent and discerning contemporaries. His mood was unpredictable. His relationship with Euphemia was

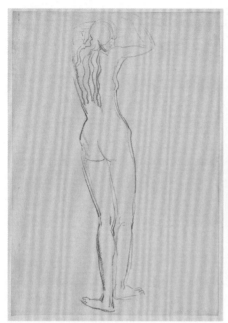 

Left: Jacob Epstein, *Study for a fountain figure (Euphemia Lamb)*, 1911, crayon on paper, 50.8 x 35.5 cm
Right: Jacob Epstein, plaster cast of *Fountain Figure* (Garden Statue), *c.* 1911

stormy – they were both passionate and capricious. Had he been of a different disposition, their relationship might have lasted longer and Euphemia wouldn't have had to survive in Paris in the way she did. Although their relationship lasted less than a year – they married in May 1906 and it was over by May 1907 – they kept in touch and remained friends and possibly lovers. We have seen that Henry Lamb took some responsibility for Euphemia when she was spiralling out of control in Paris, by writing to Roché in December 1907 and by going to Paris in August 1908 to fetch her back to London. In 1909 the pair of them visited their cottage in Wiltshire. Because they didn't divorce until 1928, their lives remained intertwined for some years.

Without Henry Lamb there would have been no Euphemia Lamb; Nina Forrest would have had a different life. The letter is a touching tribute to Euphemia and her genius. Two restless souls whose brief alliance had catalysed something in each of them and catapulted them both into extraordinary lives.

TWELVE

Legacy

Only very recently have histories of nineteenth- and twentieth-century painting paid much attention to models as collaborators of avant garde artists and in some way the participants in the creation of modern art.[1] – Colin Bailey

THE MODERNIST MOVEMENT REQUIRED emancipated women to support it. The portraits of Euphemia narrate the journey of one woman at the beginning of the twentieth century who carved out for herself an independent and creative life. Euphemia Lamb was an ordinary girl who became a bohemian. Becoming a bohemian was like undergoing a physical operation where you were surgically removed from your previous life, family and background and flung from the English provinces into the playgrounds of Europe. How did she achieve this? Her beauty was part of the offer, to attract Henry Lamb and make a successful career as an artist's model. But beauty is not enough to explain the wide range of artists and writers she inspired. There has to be another ingredient, and I think this is to be found in her unusual and outlandish personality. Euphemia had the ability to immerse herself fully in any environment and to hustle herself upwards through society. This transgressive quality, combined with her intelligence, beauty and apparent insouciance captured the imagination of the artists and writers she inspired. As a model she brought about Henry Lamb's vocation as an artist, but she was more than a model. Euphemia's special talent as a model was her ability to withstand the scrutiny of the male gaze and not become a victim of it. In fact, she embraced the male gaze and it empowered her. In all her portraits and photographs she seems completely comfortable and at

---

1. Colin Bailey, 'In Plain Sight', *New York Review of Books*, 66, no. 20, December 2019.

ease with herself and her body. A muse is someone who captures the spirit of the age, as well as the energy of the artist. Euphemia's energy and freedom enthralled the artists she met.

Virginia Woolf wrote:

> 'On the one hand is truth, on the other there is personality. And if we think of truth as something of granite-like solidity and of personality as something rainbow like intangibility.'

Woolf was writing about biography, but the argument applies equally well to art: there is the beauty (truth) and then there is the personality. How these two qualities are welded together determines the truth of inner life and brings a work of art to life. Lisa Tickner raised the question of women's contribution to modernism and argued for a wider definition to include enablers, patrons and editors as well as artists. She sees the models as an active agent of art history. She also wrote of Augustus John being dependent on the inspiration of his models:

> '… before the inscrutable beauty of a few women he could lose and renew himself'.[2]

Germaine Greer theorised the idea of a muse:

> 'A muse's job is to penetrate the male artist and bring forth a work from the womb of his mind.'

Greer argues that a muse is not just a paid model, she is, in fact, in her purest aspect, the feminine part of the male artist with which he must have intercourse if he is to bring into being a new work. Physical congress with the muse is not essential, as her role is to penetrate the mind and not the body. There is a tendency to conflate the idea of model and muse because of the collaboration involved. As we have seen with Euphemia, sexual intercourse was often, but not always, a

2. Lisa Tickner, '"Augustus's Sister": Gwen John, Wholeness, Harmony and Radiance', 2004.

Photograph of Euphemia Lamb and Augustus John, 1956

feature of her collaborations with artists but it was her glorious energy of character and courage that created the magic and the mystery which determined her success as a muse.

When Augustus John was an old man, he sat next to the novelist Penelope Fitzgerald at a Chelsea dinner party; he was gruff and said very little. Penelope then described how, when she asked him about Euphemia, he suddenly lit up and waxed lyrical about how wonderful and extraordinary she had been. Beauty is transient, personality is not. Augustus John continued to paint his wife Ida long after her death. It was his memory and internal version of her he was depicting.

One of the key questions in writing about Euphemia's life is how much agency she actually had. In Paris, after Henry Lamb's desertion of her, she went into freefall and led a manic and precarious existence. As Maynard Keynes commented, 'Euphemia had more of a sex life than the rest of us put together.' But she survived and she learned to tame her wild lifestyle and slow down. There is evidence of her educating herself intellectually through her exposure to ideas and books (interestingly, several of the images in this book show Euphemia reading). There is also evidence that she developed emotionally too. Euphemia was a teenager when she went to Paris, she was twenty-one years old on her return to London. This is an important time of adolescent development when the follies of youth settle down into a more mature way of living.

Euphemia was constantly seeking adventure and excitement. She was living a life that very few women of her period would have had the chance to live. The elopement and the emigration to Paris freed her of many societal constraints. The expat's liminal position was liberating for her. I think the fact that she made choices and did not stay tethered to just one artist is evidence of her agency and being in control. Her appointment of who she would go home with each evening by the giving of the bottle of milk to carry is an example of this. In his biography of Augustus John, Michael Holroyd wrote about Euphemia 'living her life through men'. Men were essential to her way of life. Most of the artists of the period were men; they were not only her lovers but her employers. She needed men to survive financially but not emotionally. Aleister Crowley captured this quality when he wrote:

'I see that she was in reality acting like an adept, keeping the planes well apart.'

Once Euphemia returned to London, she was able to slow down and reinvent herself as a professional artist's model and set about her life with some discipline and begin her journey to becoming a lady. She was comfortable living outside the patriarchal notions and norms of happiness. Agency is the sense of having a feeling of control over one's actions and their consequences. Her professionalism as both a model and as a café hostess ensured her financial stability. Many similarly beautiful models and muses met a more tragic end – one thinks of lives ravaged by drug addiction and suicide, such as Lizzie Siddal and Lilian Shelley. Euphemia avoided this fate and did not succumb to a destructive way of life. She settled down with her second husband Ned Grove and travelled the world. After her divorce, she became a farmer, stayed in touch with her artist friends and collected art. Some eccentricities remained: in Paris she had a collection of toy animals, at Stoke, her Hampshire manor house, she had a coterie of real farm animals and at her death she owned over twenty-five dogs.

Euphemia was an exceptional woman who took her life into her own hands by reinventing herself in Paris and defined herself against the grain of mainstream society. She lives on in the art and the written works she inspired.

Jean Cocteau, in *Praising the Muse*, wrote:

'One should render homage to the profound and sparkling women who live in the shade of the men of their epoch and who, within the artist's world through the simple fact that they emanate a radiance more beautiful than necklaces, exert an occult influence.'[3]

This is my homage to Euphemia.

3. Jean Cocteau, *Praising the Muse*, 1953, in his introduction to *Misia and the Muses* by Misia Sert.

Don Juan et la Petite Sirène[1]

ONE AFTERNOON AT THE END OF SUMMER, Don Juan was walking by the sea. Under the sun the sky was blue and the long sandy beach wove its way between the crashing waves and the silent clumps of green pines. Don Juan walked on the hard sand just on the edge of the waves, an occasional wave would spread out its slippery skirt and wet the soles of his feet. He remembered how as a child he would look at the ever-changing sea without becoming weary. He loved it when it was smooth and fear aggravated his love when it was rough. He sensed his eye running along the path of bygone days; the waves rising impenetrably towards the open ocean and reaching the horizon which no longer told him anything.

Suddenly from the waves rose a cherry stone pressed from your fingers, a small white and green being whose movements left a stripe on the sand. The figure had white and pearly skin from the sea. Like two small kidneys, two tendrils were attached to her thighs and rubbed the ground. Two long mobile tails were attached to her fins.

'A little mermaid,' exclaimed Don Juan.

'You said it,' she replied.

She raised herself aloft on her little arms and moving her tails advanced towards him clumsily. Her head was upright, her complexion striking. She stared at Don Juan with watery blue eyes. Her red mouth was upturned and her rich convex lips were like a double headed flower. Don Juan stared at her intently.

Without turning round, she laughed at him irreverently and he felt

---

1. *Don Juan and the Small Mermaid.*

embarrassed. Her small teeth shone and her two tails wriggled with joy. Don Juan found it so funny that he burst out laughing with side splitting intensity. Once the laughter subsided the pair became friends. Immediately she started singing a fashionable tune which she must have picked up swimming around one of the tourist boats. Her wide open eyes were full of intense wonder.

'So what are we going to play?' she asked as she dragged herself towards the dry sand.

'Lend me your coat so I can sit down on it?'

Don Juan proffered his coat. She spread it out with an absurd gesture. He noticed her supple neck where the scales began and thought of her sexual orifices as fresh gills. She sat down.

'Today is my birthday,' she teased with lying duplicitous eyes.

'The only day of the year when I can lift my tails.'

'Help me!'

From her hips she pushed down the scaly flaps and rolled them with difficulty down to her knees.

'Grab my fins and hold tight!'

Don Juan pulled and the tails came off like boots. And beneath revealed a pair of legs which belonged to her.

She laughed and turned over on to her back; Agitatedly she lifted her tail/legs into the air and touched them as if they were new.

Don Juan stood in front of her; he wondered how innocent this foreplay was? She folded her legs beneath her and asked,

'What's your name?'

'Don Juan – And you?'

'I am the daughter of the King of the Sea.'

'Does he have many daughters?'

'Oh yes,' and laughed fatuously.

'Are you the most beautiful one?'

'Of course.'

'How do you know?'

'Everyone does what I want. My husband, even the husbands of my sisters.'

'You are already married?'

'My husband is the Director General of the Seaweed forest for my father, the King.'

'Little Mermaid.'

'Give me a new name, an animal's name?'

'Little seal.'

She grabbed the head of Don Juan and gently kissed his lips. She stood up and danced a jig and then somersaulted on the sand.

'Little seal. Little seal,' she exclaimed.

She picked up her two tails and carried them in one arm and dragged his coat with the other.

'Let's go into the woods, do you want to?'

She galloped along, zigzagging the coat behind her. Don Juan followed her and made sure not to step on the coat. He was mesmerised by her pretty back covered with golden sand, scampering away from him. He could still taste her lips and her touch on his mouth.

She galloped away like someone unused to solid ground, jumping ineffectually into the air. He was worried that she would crash into a tree trunk mistaking it for a piece of seaweed from her father's underwater forest. She moved through the tightly packed trees and snake-like roots, letting out a merry little war cry. The coat became caught, she tripped and crashed to the ground. She was laughing, lying on the ground next to an old pine tree weeping its resin. She landed onto a carpet of yellow pine needles and a thin layer of moss. She scrutinised him and then gestured for Don Juan to join her.

She took his long hand and examined it like a landscape; her fingers followed the network of swollen veins and arrived upon a scar.

'What's this?' she demanded.

'An old sword cut.'

She stuck her mouth onto the scar and threw her arms around Don Juan's neck and pulled his head towards her, rubbing it against her face and neck. Into his ear she whispered,

'You are a good man, you are strong. You could tear me apart with your hands. I am scared of you.'

It was not true that she was afraid. She nibbled his cheek and stroked his back and then kissed him in the cavity of his ear. The kiss resounded and rung out. Her eye lids were now half shut and she let herself go.

'Your turn now.'

Don Juan leaned his face towards her white shoulder, he could smell the strong scent of resin.

The little mermaid no longer felt like a fish but like a girl in the sun. Don Juan examined her body. So well formed and undulating. His eyes followed her slopes and arrived at her white tummy and the tuft of golden hair and sped towards her feet.

'To have such beauty in one's hands without any struggle. Such abandonment.'

He pondered and raised his hands towards the branches and the sky.

The little mermaid put her elbows onto his face and burst into tears. Her cries pierced the air and her little tummy convulsed with sobs. She screamed like a child, high pitched without drawing for breath.

Don Juan couldn't stand it and stopped laughing. She raised her arms from his face and a rare grimace appeared on her. With her mouth open, drawn down, the creases of despair rose to her nose. Her forehead humped above her eyebrows and her eyes were held down with the backs of her forefingers to spread out the tears.

Don Juan found her adorable and remained motionless.

'I am ugly and horrid.'

She could tell from Don Juan's eyes that he didn't believe this. She pushed her young torso forwards and enveloped him with her legs.

'I won't help and I won't hinder,' he thought.

She turned him over and mounted him and from her mouth showered him with kisses. She rubbed her gentle breasts into his face.

Don Juan began to become involved.

Stretching out and climbing on top of him, she spread her weight and lay flat aloft him.

Don Juan now took charge. She sensed him and like a cat began to violate him.

'All right,' he thought, he made an effort, rolled his eyes and complied. He had the upper hand.

She became immobile and watched his face; Seeing the storm penetrate she was amazed that her beauty terrified him. She caressed his shoulder;

he made crosses with his fingers in the sand. They had not known each other very long. The silence was like the fog without the wind.

'What am I going to do with the little seal now?' he thought.

With her long dangling hair, her profile disappeared. He could only see a narrow face and her round skull. Don Juan looked out to the sea and stifled a yawn. Her mouth tightened and frowned. Out of nowhere, she suddenly threw a handful of sand into his face. He closed his eyes in time but not his mouth; he jumped up and spat out the sand.

'Little seal this is silly.'

She was rooting around on the ground; she found what she was looking for; it was a dead branch. She raised it above him and broke the sticks across his legs in one blow. He grabbed her guilty hand but with her spare hand she scratched his neck with her sharp nails, narrowly missing his eyes. He caught her other hand and held both her wrists. They were face to face staring at each other. She wanted to kill him; he was distracted and she bit his forearm as if it were a loaf. Don Juan stepped back and without letting go made a sharp jolt to one side. Her frail shoulders cracked and she rolled onto the sand. Genuine tears rolled down her cheeks. Kneeling, her broken arms hung down and she looked at Don Juan. With a cruel air he felt justified in his action.

'Oh Don Juan I know I am so wicked. I have hurt you and you have hurt me. I'll never do it again. I love you because you have beaten me. It is all the fault of my husband. He allows me to do anything; The King, my uncle...'

'Liar,' interrupted Don Juan.

She looked up and rested her chin against him and offered her lips humbly.

Don Juan felt that he had never tasted that mouth. He took the little creature into his arms and cradled her gently, he kissed her sighing mouth and her injured shoulders. The little mermaid closed her eyes with the gentle rocking motion and snuggled into him. She purred. She must have been tired after her exertions on terra firma and the recent battle and she fell instantly asleep.

Don Juan held her on top of him like a child and looked contemplatively at her pale face. Such confidence, how right she had been to want to beat him because he didn't love her enough. In her sleep she was embalmed like a field of ripe wheat. Her weight moved as she breathed in and out. He repositioned her numb leg and in so doing her sleeping face came nearer to his eyes.

'The milk of your skin, the flour of your skin, which I touch with my mouth. Your golden eyelash is swimming there. Your red mouth is closed and your nostrils are breathing. I have a feeling of vertigo. I feel as if I could fall into your face as if in one's dreams one falls into the sky.'

The lips of Don Juan grazed timidly at her whiteness. He was afraid of the overly blue eyes which were unpredictable but they didn't open. Her cheeks glowed red from inside or from their kissing. There was a complicity in her lithe body. Don Juan buzzed with emotion and a sudden respect for her. Her blue eyes did not open but she raised her arms a little to embrace him. And love having passed, they remained side by side without a word. Through the branches the sun went down. When it was at the point where the sky met the sea, the little mermaid murmured,

'When the sun touches the water, I shall have to put my tails back on and enter the sea … unless…'

'Unless what?' he replied.

Don Juan felt an old aversion to carrying baggage. The little mermaid stared at him. He saw her blue eyes get bigger and wondered whether she would attack him. Her tense red lips gave a piercing whistle and a contemptuous laugh. She trotted out her worst insults and all the foul language she had learned from the sailors. When she had exhausted one language she switched to another but made a number of mistakes.

'Help me put on my tail.'

'There are other women on earth more beautiful than me…?'

'Help your little seal back into the water.'

As he did this her feet sank deeper and deeper into the soft sand. Don Juan managed to bend so as to keep her soft mouth against his.

Just as they reached the horizon he felt the sensation of the irreparable being mixed with relief and he threw her back into the sea.

FIN

Two Poems by Aleister Crowley

ALEISTER CROWLEY IMMORTALISED EUPHEMIA in a poem called 'After Judgment' in his collection, *The Winged Beetle*; he calls her 'Dorothy'.

After Judgment

To Ophelia L[1]

> So! Thou has given Thy judgment, God!
>   And I am evermore accurst,
>   Cast to the blackness of the abode
>   By Thee – O Thou Who made first!
>
> Thou Who hast made me, tortured me,
>   Mocked me with life, mocked me with death,
>   Mocked me with love – O Misery
>   Of each God's death, of each Slave's breath!
>
> Yea, for that Thou didst give me her –
>   Indeed my Dorothy! the sun
>   That fires my life, the spell to stir
>   My soul's enchantments every one:

---

1. Ophelia was Euphemia's nickname given to her by Roché and Hessel.

For this I curse Thee! She was fair
    As day and brighter than the moon
  And all the gold stung in her hair;
    And all the dawn of May – and of June!–

Kindled her cheeks; her eyes were blue
    As all Thy skies, as all Thy seas.
  Her mouth – Oh God! Her mouth that slew
    Imagination's ecstasies!

For while I praised the pearl-clear skin,
    The bright lithe body's supple growth,
  By God! I could not even begin
    To say one word about her mouth!

God! Hadst Thou given me one word,
    I now might praise Thee, though Thou damn.
  But oh! Not ever a soul hath heard
    Its echo, O Thou great I am!

Lo! Thou hast made the winds, the stars,
    The sun, the moon, the great grave earth;
  Thou has touched the swaying nenuphars
    With music, and made godly mirth

With corn and wine; Thou hasn't made Thee man;
    Thou hast loved and suffered, died and risen;
  But – hath Thy mouth grown white and wan,
    Sucked out into that strange sweet prison

Nay, Thou hast never kissed the mouth
    Of Dorothy! as I!
  Thou hast never felt its eager growth
    Upon my Lesbian ecstasy.

Therefore I curse Thee not, accurst
    Who art in that one flower foregone-
And I in the last match Thee the first
    When that red mouth I fasten on

Farewell! O God, in endless bliss
    Crowned with Thine angels singing by:
I go to hell, with her last kiss
    Yet tingling in my memory.

Nay, start not from Thy throne! I go
    At Thy black damning to the deep.
Thou canst not follow me! I know
    This thing I had, and this I keep.

God! I have loved. I love! I love.
    And shall love through Thine ageless hell.
Thou hast the kingdom of the Above,
    And I, her memory. Fare Thee Well!

To Thine I am – supreme exclaim,
    The total of all that may be said!–
I answer from the abyss of flame:
    Dorothy! And her mouth was red.

'After Judgment' is an ode to love and their sex life; after Aleister left Paris he went to North Africa with Victor Neuburg. Euphemia stayed in touch with Crowley; her second husband, Ned Grove, was a Crowley acolyte. The second poem 'Telepathy' deals with the initiation of Victor Neuburg and Euphemia's complicity in it; a letter received from her in London seems to have inspired the poem.

Telepathy

Poem by Aleister Crowley
For Euphemia L.

From gloomy London overseas
   My lady sends a letter.
My credit's gone: the Deity
   May write me down a debtor,
For I had thought I was free–
   I find I have a fetter!

    Yea; must some god announce afresh
    No more they are twain; they are
      One flesh?

For here I sit and laugh and smoke
   And play with youth and pleasure;
Life is a dream, and death a joke,
   And love is a thing of leisure–
The dance is done, the spell is broke,
   And marred the merry measure!

    Yes; my small kiss is somehow worth
    The love of all the boys on earth!

The shy sweet smiles, the tender eyes
   And bodies slim that woo me;
The sobs, the sighs, the throbs, the cries
   Of love are nothing to me.
My lady's magic madness flies
   Like poison through and through me!

Yea, love; my echo is as loud
As all the cries of all the crowd.

The shaft of love she shot in May
Still rankles in September;
The flames in June that died away
Have yet a lively ember.
I force myself to dream all day:
Night wakes me – I remember.

Yea; in the night thou lackest me.
And I? Ah surely I lack thee!

I must remember how we stood
And let mad Paris pass us
(Holding one moment to be good
For all the years surpass us.)
And touched in our beatitude
The peak of Mount Parnassus.

Yea; we did well to break the bars,
And dwell one moment with the stars!

We played the ancient comedy
That Pan taught to the Satyrs
We slew the victim rightfully;
We tore his soul to tatters,
Still laughing through the tragedy–
We knew that nothing matters!

Yea; fitted that strange play of Pan
For Gods and fiends; but not for man!

Unless – unless – unless – unless
   Our priestly hands were steaming
With other life (sweet murderess!)
   That his that lay there screaming
Between our knives – Or blood! Confess
   The truth; or am I dreaming?

     Yes floating on that cold pale flood
     Were two red stars of our own blood.

We left our laugh, a smouldering coal
   Upon his naked middle:
We ravelled out his love; we stole
   His heart-strings for our fiddle:
Strange tortured music from his soul
   We wrung, a writhing riddle!

     Yea; our mouths took a subtle curve
     As we devoured him nerve by nerve.

We danced, obscenely delicate
   The dance of cup and thyrsus
We made him love, we made him hate,
   We made him bless and curse us
Yea, O my darling, we were Fate.
   Then how should Fate reverse us?

     Yea, love; how cruelly we played
     With the poor worm we had made!

It cannot be (it cannot be!)
　That we ourselves are taken
In the sweet snare, my Dorothy!
　Did Love, true love, awaken?
And, even so, dear, why should we
　Be wildly wit-forsaken?

　　Yea; for we digged a wanton pit.
　　Ourselves are fallen into it.

Our dance grew fierce – self stirred, self willed
　And Bacchus shewed his forehead
Jutting sharp horns; his grape distilled
　A liquor harsh and florid.
Our cool sweet kisses throbbed and thrilled
　From temperate to torrid.

　　Yes; the new wine burns up our brain.
　　Like molten gold our kisses rain.

The month of love has curled our lips
　In tense perverted fancies;
Our eyes were sunk in black eclipse
　To rise in glittering trances;
Our belly-muscles tight as whips
　By dint of Arab dances!

　　Yea; all our love is glittering steel
　　Sharpened on torture's aching wheel.

My Dorothy! my Dorothy!
  Our mouths were wried and bleeding.
Love's eucharistic mystery!
  Their suckling lips were feeding
At the black breasts of ecstasy,
  Of ecstasy exceeding!

Yes; at the paps of Isis we
    Drained starry milk of ecstasy.

O thou close-fitted to my soul,
  Close fitted to my skin,
Moving as one delicious whole
  Without us and within!
How have we lost the iron control
  That curbed and spurred our sin?

    Yes; like one snake's death spasm we were
    How taken in the serpent snare?

Indeed, indeed blind fools we passed
  From light and light's dominion
To some black cavern of the vast
  On some demonic pinion.
And here we lie – discrowned at last –
  A monarch grown a minion.

    Yes; we are come from the bright God
    To some most desolate abode.

Or is it crowned, thrice crowned, we are?
   Crowned with long thorns sharp gleaning.
So that bright blood jets out afar
   From starry brains a-streaming?
Yea! In our night there shines a star
   Beyond our dearest dreaming.

     Yea; there is born a fearful light
     Proceeding from the Infinite.

However that may be, 'tis clear
   What duty bids endeavour:
To find you out in London dear, –
   A 'now' is worth a 'never'! –
To make to-day a heaven of cheer,
   And make to-day 'for ever'!

     Yea; though we know how springs run
     We'll trust our future, you and I.

Ah, madman! Was there ever yet
   A love that lived a lustre
That's the last folly, to forget,
   To cling to her, to trust her!
She's but one star – supremely set,
   I grant! – but in a cluster!

     Yea; we may tire; the sea holds yet
     More fish than ever came to net!

Acknowledgements

I WOULD LIKE TO THANK Joanna Scanlan for setting me on the trail of Augustus John and James Dickson Innes, which led to my discovery of Euphemia. And to Janina Ramirez and Wendy Jones who encouraged me to pursue my research and write about her. I would like to thank all the archivists who have helped me find relevant letters and diaries; the Tate Archives; the Harry Ransom Center and the Carlton Lake archive at the University of Texas, Austin (with extra special thanks to Courtney Welu); King's College Library, Cambridge; Fitzwilliam Museum, Cambridge; Ashmolean Museum, Oxford; National Museum of Wales; National Library of Wales; Sheffield Art Gallery; Poole Museums; Salisbury Museum; British Library; Huntingdon Library, Pasadena; Berg Collection, New York Public Library.

I am grateful to Lady Antonia Fraser for her memories of her uncle, Henry Lamb, and to Lady Emma Monson for her memories of her grandfather Francis MacNamara and permission to use her portrait of him. Many thanks to the other private collectors who have given me permission to use their drawings of Euphemia and to the dealers and auction houses who helped me find them.

Howard Walwyn and Felix Obholzer helped me translate the short stories of Roché and Hessel from the original French and German. I was helped with my research on James Dickson Innes by John Hoole, and Osian Gwyn invited me to Rhyd y Fen, the farmhouse and inn where Innes and John stayed on their first trip to Arenig.

Thanks to my readers, Paul Dean, Jonathan Randall, Luke Farey, Martin Newman, Lynne Roberts and Juliet Rosenfield for their comments and advice, and to my editor Imogen Palmer.

Picture Credits

Many thanks to the following institutions for images:

p2 and p38 collection & image © Hugh Lane Gallery / © Estate of the Artist / © Estate of Henry Lamb / Messums: 'Reproduced by kind permission of the Henry Lamb estate, C/o Messums Org

pp 8, 64, 68, 70, 71, 75, 76, Carlton Lake Literary File Photography Collection. Harry Ransom Center, The University of Texas at Austin.

p14 private collection, @image courtesy of Henry Lamb estate and Salisbury Museum,

p15 The Henry Lamb Estate, image courtesy of Messums Org

p18 © Estate of Augustus John. All rights reserved 2024 / Bridgeman Images

p20 photo © The Maas Gallery, London / © Estate of Henry Lamb. All rights reserved 2024 / Bridgeman Images

p21 (left) Ian Dagnall Computing / Alamy Stock Photo

p21 (right) courtesy of Wikimedia Commons

p25 private Collection © Image courtesy of Roseberys Fine Art Auctioneers & Valuers. Courtesy of Henry Lamb estate

p27 photo © The Maas Gallery, London / © Estate of Augustus John. All rights reserved 2024 / Bridgeman Images

p31 private collection

p32 © Manchester Art Gallery / Bridgeman Images

p33 Historic Images / Alamy Stock Photo

p34 courtesy of Wikimedia Commons

p35 private collection

p37 © Tate

p41 and front cover © Estate of Augustus John. All rights reserved 2024 / Bridgeman Images

p42 courtesy of Wikimedia Commons

p45 Estate of Henry Lamb / © Ashmolean Museum, University of Oxford

p46 private collection

p51 private collection

p53 © National Museums Liverpool

p56 © Estate of Augustus John. All rights reserved 2024 / Bridgeman Images

p59 photo © Agnew's, London / © Estate of Augustus John. All rights reserved 2024 / Bridgeman Images

p61 courtesy of Browse & Darby

p63 Sueddeutsche Zeitung Photo / Alamy Stock Photo

Index

Published in 2025 by Unicorn
an imprint of Unicorn Publishing Group
Charleston Studio
Meadow Business Centre
Lewes
BN8 5RW
www.unicornpublishing.org

ISBN 978-1-916846-71-5
10 9 8 7 6 5 4 3 2 1

Design by Felicity Price-Smith
Printed in Turkey by Fine Tone Ltd